LESSONS IN TEACHING
COMPUTING
IN PRIMARY SCHOOLS

Sara Miller McCune founded SAGE Publishing in 1965 to support the dissemination of usable knowledge and educate a global community. SAGE publishes more than 1000 journals and over 800 new books each year, spanning a wide range of subject areas. Our growing selection of library products includes archives, data, case studies and video. SAGE remains majority owned by our founder and after her lifetime will become owned by a charitable trust that secures the company's continued independence.

Los Angeles | London | New Delhi | Singapore | Washington DC | Melbourne

REVISED & UPDATED EDITION

LESSONS IN TEACHING
COMPUTING
IN PRIMARY SCHOOLS

JAMES BIRD, HELEN CALDWELL & PETER MAYNE

https:// SECOND EDITION

SAGE | LearningMatters

Learning Matters
An imprint of SAGE Publications Ltd
1 Oliver's Yard
55 City Road
London EC1Y 1SP

SAGE Publications Inc.
2455 Teller Road
Thousand Oaks, California 91320

SAGE Publications India Pvt Ltd
B 1/I 1 Mohan Cooperative Industrial Area
Mathura Road
New Delhi 110 044

SAGE Asia-Pacific Pte Ltd
3 Church Street
#10-04 Samsung Hub
Singapore 049483

Editor: Amy Thornton
Development editor: Geoff Barker
Production controller: Chris Marke
Project management: Swales & Willis Ltd, Exeter,
Devon
Marketing manager: Lorna Patkai
Cover design: Wendy Scott
Typeset by: C&M Digitals (P) Ltd, Chennai, India
Printed and bound by
CPI Group (UK) Ltd, Croydon, CR0 4YY

First published in 2014 by Learning Matters Ltd

Second edition 2017

Library of Congress Control Number: 2016960205

British Library Cataloguing in Publication Data

A catalogue record for this book is available from the
British Library

ISBN: 978-1-4739-7040-3
ISBN: 978-1-4739-7041-0 (pbk)

At SAGE we take sustainability seriously. Most of our products are printed in the UK using FSC papers and boards.
When we print overseas we ensure sustainable papers are used as measured by the PREPS grading system.
We undertake an annual audit to monitor our sustainability.

Contents

The authors and contributors

James Bird (author) is a senior lecturer at the School of Education, Oxford Brookes University. He was involved with the Royal Academy of Engineering/British Computer Society consultation for the new computing curriculum. James worked for 25 years in primary and higher education as a teacher and technology in learning specialist. He combines two professional roles, working part-time in university and also as a school improvement officer in a multi-academy trust.

Helen Caldwell (author) is a senior lecturer at the University of Northampton, where she is curriculum lead for primary computing in ITE (Initial Teacher Education) and programme lead for the PG Certificate in Primary Computing. Her teaching covers the use of technology across primary subjects, implementing the computing curriculum and assistive technologies for SEND (special educational needs and disabilities). Helen was a member of the Computing in Initial Teacher Training Expert Group and currently sits on the ITTE National Executive Committee. Earlier roles included the post of assistive technology advisor for Milton Keynes Council and regional manager for the Open University Vital programme. Her research interests include eLearning and social networking in higher education, and computing and digital literacy in primary education.

Other SAGE books:

Caldwell H and Cullingford-Agnew, S (2017, publication pending) *Technology for SEND in Primary Schools: A Good Practice Guide*. London: SAGE.

Caldwell, H and Smith, N (2016) *Computing Unplugged: Exploring Primary Computing through Practical Activities Away from the Computer*. London: SAGE.

Caldwell, H and Bird, J (2015) *Teaching with Tablets*. London: SAGE.

Mark Dorling (contributor) has extensive primary and secondary teaching experience and has worked in industry as a computer scientist. He is a visiting lecturer at Brunel University Education Department and his work as a teacher included leading the introduction of computing into KS3 and KS4 and developing the internationally recognised Digital Schoolhouse project, a KS2 to KS3 computing-focused transition project (featured in the Royal Society Report, and which won a *Times Educational Supplement* award in 2013). Mark is on the Board of Management for Computing At School, and is their National Continuing Professional Development Coordinator, responsible for the Computing At School Master Teacher programme funded by the Department for Education.

Sway Grantham (@ SwayGrantham) (contributor) is a primary school teacher and a Specialist Leader in Education (SLE) for the Milton Keynes area. She has been ICT/Computing Leader since her NQT year and during this time has written a new curriculum and conducted research into the impact of 1:1 iPads in the primary classroom. Sway has been using technology all her life and has spent the last five years applying this to education. She was invited as a 'lead learner' to attend the first ever Raspberry Picademy, becoming a Raspberry Pi Certified Teacher, and loves the opportunities these cheap computers offer. Recently having qualified as a Google Certified Teacher, Sway believes in offering children a range of ICT and computing opportunities. Over the years, Sway has built up a successful blog **(www. swaygrantham.co.uk)**, which is full of learning ideas and pedagogy for computing, ICT and many other curriculum areas.

Alison Hannah has over 20 years of teaching and leadership experience, including roles as an advanced skills teacher, subject leader, lead practitioner, ITT associate lecturer and now assistant principal. She has lived through and worked within the many and varied developments of our education system. As assistant principal at South Devon University Technical College, she is focused on the promotion of the college specialisms in computing, science and engineering and the development of twenty-first-century lifelong learners who are competent, skilled, knowledgeable and creative.

Peter Mayne (author) is currently a senior lecturer in primary education at the University of Worcester, where he is curriculum leader for computing. He has many years' experience as a primary school teacher, ICT subject leader and deputy head teacher. His experience includes an international perspective. He has been a primary school teacher in Germany and assistant principal of a primary school in Australia. Throughout his career Peter has implemented many initiatives focusing on how technology can provide opportunities to enhance teaching and learning.

Adam Scribbans (contributor) worked as a primary teacher in a range of roles for ten years. He worked for Computing At School as National Primary Coordinator, following which he returned to a previous career of yachting and running a yacht charter company in Hampshire.

Foreword

The publication of the second edition of *Lessons in Teaching Computing in Primary Schools* provides an opportunity to stop and reflect upon national and international initiatives and technological developments to promote and develop computing in a creative way within the primary curriculum since the book was first published. National initiatives include the development of Computing At School primary hubs, the growth of Code Clubs, the BBC micro:bit, the Barefoot Computing programme, which promotes computational thinking within a primary context, and *Computational Thinking: A Guide for Teachers* (2015). International initiatives include Learn to Code Code to Learn, the Hour of Code and Europe Code Week. Technological developments include the use of tablets and age-appropriate apps to support coding and problem solving, an increased choice of educational robots to support the curriculum and numerous devices for physical computing.

Since the introduction of the Computing Programmes of Study into state primary schools and its adoption by primary academies and free schools, primary teachers have sought advice and guidance as they have encouraged their pupils not only to be digital consumers but creators of digital content – and responsible digital citizens – as well as promoting the beauty and joy of computer science. This has been achieved with the use of unplugged kinaesthetic activities to promote computer science concepts: contextualising computer science as a tool to solve real-life problems; the development and promotion of computational thinking across the curriculum; programming educational robots; engagement with physical computing; and using appropriate programming environments and activities to teach pupils the fundamentals of programming and out-of-class learning, such as clubs and competitions.

Primary teachers are recognising and acknowledging that the subject 'computing' consists of three strands: computer science, information technology and digital literacy. They are utilising appropriate resources, technologies and activities to promote these strands with pupils. As an educator and Secretary of ITTE, I am excited about this book because it advocates a creative approach to teaching the three strands of computing. Teachers are encouraged to enthuse their pupils to view technology as a tool for problem solving the challenges they are presented with and to use appropriate approaches to achieve the desired results.

From a primary teacher's perspective, the challenge as a generalist is how to include (initially) all forms of ICT – and now computing – in a world where there are competing demands on the curriculum. Within a primary school, subjects rarely exist within silos and the overarching challenge is how to embed computing thematically while at the same time teaching it specifically. In addition, teachers as professionals were, and are, faced with the challenge of translating and contextualising the Computing Programmes of Study into the primary classroom as they understand and articulate a new vocabulary and promote computer science principles and concepts. While it is acknowledged that aspects of computer science existed in the previous ICT curriculum, i.e. control and modelling, acquiring the specific subject knowledge needed to teach the subject is demanding for many teachers.

Among the challenges that primary teachers continue to face in delivering the computing curriculum are:

- What approaches should I use in teaching computing?

- How do I fit this into a demanding curriculum?

- How do I teach computing in a creative way?

- How do I engage pupils in problem solving when coding?; How do pupils develop perseverance when the code does not work?

- How do I encourage my pupils to be responsible digital citizens?

This book provides timely advice, guidance and strategies in helping teachers address these challenges.

In reading this book and visiting the companion website, I have seen old ideas revitalised and refreshed within a new context and learnt new approaches to teaching computing. The book and website are resources that I will revisit for inspiration and guidance in teaching computing in a creative way as the pedagogy continues to refine, resources are produced and new approaches articulated. I hope that you will find the same, whether as experienced teachers, educators who support primary teachers in embedding computing in the primary curriculum, or those training to teach computing in primary schools.

Andrew Csizmadia
Senior Lecturer in Computer Science Education at
Newman University
Secretary of ITTE

Acknowledgements

Every effort has been made to trace the copyright holders and to obtain their permission for the use of copyright material. The publisher and author will gladly receive any information enabling them to rectify any error or omission in subsequent editions.

The authors wish to thank Scratch for their help. Scratch is developed by the Lifelong Kindergarten Group at the MIT Media Lab. See **http://scratch.mit.edu**

Chapter 1

Algorithms and computational thinking in KS1

apply the fundamental principles of computer science

Learning outcomes

This chapter looks at how to develop pupils' understanding of algorithms and computational thinking and how this may relate to the use of technology in the wider world.

By the end of this chapter you should be able to:

- develop an understanding of the terms algorithm and computational thinking;
- develop an awareness of how computational thinking can be embedded in good primary school practice.

Teachers' Standards

Working through this chapter will help you meet the following standards:

3a. Have a secure knowledge of the relevant subject(s) and curriculum areas, foster and maintain pupils' interest in the subject, and address misunderstandings.
4b. Promote the love of learning and pupils' intellectual curiosity.

Links to the National Curriculum

Pupils should learn to:

- understand what algorithms are and how they are implemented on digital devices; and that programs execute by following precise and unambiguous instructions;
- recognise common uses of technology beyond school.

Introduction

Although terminology is used for clarification, it can also be a hindrance to embracing new ideas. The terms algorithm and computational thinking are not new and don't have to represent difficult concepts, but used in connection with young pupils for the first time they may cause some anxiety.

The purpose of this chapter is to demystify these terms and consider how we can meet the National Curriculum Programme of Study requirement for pupils in Key Stage 1 (KS1) to *understand what algorithms are and how they are implemented on digital devices; and that programs execute by following precise and unambiguous instructions* (DfE, 2013). The focus is on meeting the statutory requirement in a manner which professionals would consider manageable, appropriate for the age range and embedded in good practice. This can be achieved without the need for 'expert' knowledge and even in many cases without the need to use a computer!

The New Collins Concise English Dictionary (2011) defines algorithms as any *method or procedure of computation, usually a series of steps.*

Computational thinking should be seen as a problem-solving process, which incorporates the use of algorithms by analysing and logically organising data.

Lesson idea: introducing algorithms

This lesson focus is on algorithms being a sequence of precise instructions and related to the need for digital devices also to have precise instructions, in order to follow a preset program with a predetermined outcome.

Before you start

Be clear in your own mind what an algorithm is and how the concept can be embedded in a cross-curricular way.

Pupils need to be grouped according to ability.

Things you need

- Toaster, bread, knife and margarine for the teacher demonstration.
- Laminated cards – on each card should be one of the steps for cleaning teeth (the sequence has been decomposed into smaller steps), Blu-tack, mini-whiteboards.

Context

After an initial teacher demonstration, this particular lesson plan focuses on creating an algorithm for cleaning teeth, which would link well to personal, social, health and economic education, and with a topic on 'All About Me'. The principle of this lesson could also be used in many different contexts, for example, crossing a road, making a sandwich, getting dressed.

Learning objectives

- To understand the term 'algorithm'.

- To understand the precise nature of algorithms.

- To understand that algorithms provide the precise instructions for common digital devices.

Lesson outline

In order for pupils to understand the term 'algorithm', they need to create some of their own and try them out in the physical sense. This all takes place away from a computer but is related back to digital devices.

Class introduction

The pupils are told that today their teacher is a robot and needs to be programmed to make some toast. Can the class help?

The teacher needs to follow the exact instructions the pupils give. It is important to be pedantic and petty. Relate this to the need for any digital device to have precise instructions. Throughout the lesson be aware of the language you use: the term algorithm is very likely to be new to them but they may also need help understanding words such as precise and clear. It is important not to make assumptions about pupils' understanding of language.

> ### Commentary
>
> Model the instructions using the toaster and write the final solution to make one slice of toast on the interactive whiteboard. A piece of toast as a reward for a group with great ideas may be well received!

One possible solution is presented below:

1. Open the packet of bread.

2. Take one slice of bread out with your hand.

3. Put the bread in the toaster.

4. Push the lever on the toaster down.

5. Wait until the toast pops up.

6. Take the toast out of the toaster with your hand.

7. Get a plate.

8. With your hand, put the toast on the plate.

9. Get a knife and margarine.

10. With one hand holding the tub of margarine, use the other to take the lid off the margarine.

11. Put the knife into the margarine and put some margarine on it.

12. Hold the plate with your left hand.

13. With the knife in your right hand, spread the margarine on the toast.

14. Put the lid on the margarine.

15. Pick the toast up in your hand.

16. Eat the toast.

17. End.

The sequence above is not the only answer, but whatever solution the pupils decide should be modelled on the interactive whiteboard. It is possible to be even more precise than the above solution. The algorithm could be decomposed into a whole series of further steps (for example, about the process of eating), but we need to assume that the human robot has some such functions already programmed into its memory.

Commentary

A development would be to ask pupils to make a decision as to whether they would like more than one slice of toast. This would involve an alternative loop, with the last four steps being:

Eat the toast > Repeat until no longer hungry for toast > If no longer hungry for toast > End

Classroom organisation

Put the pupils into ability groups of three or four. They are to use all or a selection of the cards drawn up from the list below, depending on their ability. The most able are given a selection of cards and have to work the rest of the algorithmic sequence out. The middle-ability group are given all the cards to place in order. The less able pupils will either have adult support or be given enough cards to create the algorithm, which won't have been decomposed into as many steps.

When the cards are considered a working algorithm, the pupils should Blu-tack them to a surface.

Further differentiation might involve having bogus cards in the pack or asking the most able to complete the task without using the word 'brush'!

The following will be cut up into each step and laminated.

Algorithm for cleaning teeth (a possible solution)

- Pick up the toothbrush with your hand.
- Turn on the tap with your other hand.

- Rinse toothbrush under the tap.
- Turn off tap with your hand.
- Pick up the toothpaste tube with your hand.
- Hold the toothpaste and toothbrush in one hand.
- Unscrew toothpaste top with the other.
- Squeeze toothpaste tube.
- Squirt the toothpaste on to the brush.
- Put the toothpaste down.
- Open your mouth.
- Brush your teeth for two minutes.
- Spit into the washbasin.
- Close your mouth.
- Turn the tap on with one hand.
- Hold the toothbrush in the other hand.
- Rinse toothbrush.
- Turn the tap off.
- Put down toothbrush.
- Hold the toothpaste tube in one hand.
- Screw the top on with the other hand.
- Stop.

Peer assessment

Pupils share their algorithms with another group and they assess whether the algorithm would work.

For evidence of the pupils' work and for follow-up activities, it would be valuable to take a digital photograph of their completed algorithm. This could be uploaded to an e-journal or kept as a hard copy.

Commentary

It is important here to tell the pupils that they are considering whether the sequence actually works. Although an algorithm needs to be precise, there are many ways to complete it.

Mini-plenary

This would be an ideal opportunity to celebrate the pupils' work and discuss the solutions they have found.

The next stage of the lesson would be to introduce the idea of debugging a program. This would involve each group changing the order of four of the steps (decomposition) in the sequence and another group would need to correct (debug) the revised sequence.

Commentary

Endeavour to use the correct computational language here, for example, debug the sequence rather than correct the errors.

The teacher should ask the pupils to suggest anything in their home they think would have an algorithm to enable it to work. Examples here would be a washing machine, dishwasher, television remote control. If possible, show a simulation of a washing machine following an algorithmic process.

Plenary

The lesson ends with self-assessment. The use of mini-whiteboards may be of value here.

Rather than asking vaguely 'Do you understand today's lesson?', be more specific, such as:

1.   Write or draw an example of a digital device that uses an algorithm.

2.   If you are asked to debug something, what does that mean?

3.   What happens if an algorithm is not clear and precise?

The self-assessment questions should relate back to the learning objectives, which were:

*   to understand algorithm as a term;

*   to understand the precise nature of algorithms;

*   to understand that algorithms provide the precise instructions for common digital devices.

Finally the teacher could ask the pupils to test their algorithm out at home, possibly accessing it via an e-journal. An alternative task would be to create and then test another human algorithm. This could be done either in written or pictorial form.

Commentary

This reinforces the work in class, makes the task more meaningful and also encourages a discussion with parents about the topic.

Taking it further

The lesson idea presented helps to meet the National Curriculum requirement of *understanding what algorithms are and that programs work by following precise and unambiguous instructions*. Pupils at KS1 should also understand that algorithms can be represented in simple formats, for example, storyboards and narrative texts. It is also important for pupils to know that algorithms can describe everyday activities and can be followed by humans and computers, although computers need more precise instructions than humans (CAS, 2012).

Pupils should also be aware that steps (decomposition) within a sequence can be repeated. This was mentioned as part of the lesson introduction, but a follow-up lesson could pursue this much further. The following chapter, relating to aspects of programming, considers this more fully.

There are many very useful ideas at **code-it.co.uk** that provide opportunities to explore algorithms. These resources are all free. One example which engages children, reinforces the concept of algorithms and is easily differentiated is the 'Human Crane' activity (**http://code-it.co.uk/wp-content/uploads/2015/05/humancraneplan.pdf**). The children have to pretend that a crane has broken down and they have to move blocks in an algorithmic manner, using cards with images of the different directions on them. There are 12 such problems to solve, which are progressive in difficulty.

Barefoot computing (**http://barefootcas.org.uk**) also provides many valuable free teaching resources to support the understanding of algorithms and other aspects of primary computer science.

The weblink **http://games.thinkingmyself.com** provides an interesting child-friendly way to introduce algorithms and develop algorithmic thinking. It suggests how to make algorithms more efficient for multiple tasks and also provides an online treasure chest game following an algorithmic process.

In addition to pupils creating games in the traditional format, using computer software such as the 2Simple program, 2DIY allows them to do this in a digital manner (**www.2simple.com/2diy**). Children need to plan the sequence of steps in order for the game they have created to work.

The TES iboard (**www.iboard.co.uk/teacher/jlisaw8/1**) has some excellent sequencing games which will further enhance the understanding of the sequential process. These games link sequencing to life cycles and everyday activities. Most of the activities are straightforward, although there is a bell-ringing game that will challenge the more able.

The cleaning-teeth activity suggested earlier in this chapter has probably shown that a solution can be found in many ways. Some of these ways are more efficient than others and this can be used as a key learning point. An inefficient algorithm works, but not as quickly or effectively as the most efficient solution. The following paper-folding exercise is a good way to reinforce this.

Demonstrate how to fold a piece of paper into 16 sections and then ask the pupils to recreate the folds. When the class come back together, encourage the pupils to share their folding method and discuss any differences they have noticed. Ask the pupils to do this again and challenge them to find as many ways to fold the paper as possible. Tell them to keep a record of all the different ways there are to fold one piece of paper into 16 sections. When they have completed the task, find out how many ways they came up with. Compare the number of folds that different groups used.

This activity is useful when discussing the idea that the exact same thing can be accomplished with more or less work, depending on the method that you use. It would be useful to follow this up by thinking of other situations where an end solution can be reached in different ways. Pupils should again be encouraged to consider the most efficient way and the advantage of accomplishing something with fewer steps.

Using repetition in algorithms is a key factor in making them more efficient. This could be introduced or reinforced through instructions to make a card for whatever festival or celebration is topical at the time. The teacher could give the instructions in a very long-winded way and then in a manner that uses repetition. Just seeing the instructions written in the different ways would make the point that some algorithms are more efficient and using repetition is one means of doing this.

Activity

Consider how the introduction of algorithms could seamlessly be embedded into your lessons; remember it is likely to be more meaningful if it is introduced in a cross-curricular context.

Make a list of all the ways teaching algorithms as outlined here can support teaching and learning in other areas of the curriculum.

Discussion

The lesson outlined clearly embeds the concept of algorithms in a cross-curricular manner. It is not new for teachers to ask pupils to sequence events; for example, it forms a key part of instructional writing. So why introduce terms like algorithms and call it computing? It is also legitimate to ask what the relevance is to a child in KS1.

First, let us consider the terminology.

As regards terminology, we have focused on the use of the term algorithm and mentioned other subject-specific vocabulary in passing, but it is useful to be aware of the key vocabulary when teaching computer science. Although as teachers we need to direct the pupils to the precise vocabulary, through engaging in activities like the ones outlined, they are constructing their own understanding of computational processes. This is an excellent approach to introducing the technical terms, as the pupils already have an experience within which to relate the term. Barefoot Computing (**http://barefootcas.org.uk**) is an excellent resource for developing an understanding of the relevant computing terminology. It provides a clear explanation of all the key vocabulary in an audio form. Code-It also has a useful glossary of terminology (**http:// code-it.co.uk/csvocab**).

Sequencing, selection and repetition are part of the basic toolkit of computer programming, but they are also found in human activities such as cleaning teeth, making toast, crossing the road and many other daily activities. This is explored further in the next chapter on programming at KS1.

In order for algorithms to work in digital devices, they will not only need to be a precise set of instructions but they will also need to incorporate repetition. Many dances are a very precise set of moves (instructions) followed by repetition. The cha cha cha is a very good example of this. We may not wish to teach KS1 the cha cha cha, but there are all sorts of country and folk dances that, through precise instructions and repetitive loops, are good examples of the algorithmic process.

Technical terminology is understandable to pupils if it is used in context. To use the correct terms adds clarity and is valuable as a building block to later work. Systematic Synthetic Phonics has very successfully used the correct terminology and given pupils an understanding of vocabulary that many parents are unfamiliar with. This being the case, using a term like algorithms should be encouraged as it is well within the capability of most KS1 pupils to use it correctly and appropriately.

Second, the use of algorithms as it relates to computer science is far more than a simple list of chronological instructional writing. The writing of algorithms desires a precision of thinking, which helps pupils' conceptual development and understanding of how the digital world around them works.

Once pupils have understood the basic concept of an algorithm, it is valuable to explore their common uses. There is an algorithmic process in most games the pupils play. A treasure hunt is a navigational process of a linked list. A fun and worthwhile activity would be for the pupils initially to solve a treasure hunt and then to create their own based on algorithmic thinking. This would be best done with a precise sequence of instructions (a complex problem decomposed into simpler steps and solving this sequence one at a time). This could be completed either on a large playground grid or using a grid on paper or card. The algorithm sequence would be decomposed into a number of directional steps, for example moving squares forwards/ backwards and right/left or using the four main compass directions. There are clear, cross-curricular links here with coordinates and understanding directional terminology.

Monopoly is a circular list: in theory, the game is set up so it could never end. Snakes and Ladders uses a directional graph (Curzon, 1999). Games of this nature could be created by the pupils with a sequence of instructions, developing their understanding of algorithms and computational thinking, whilst the subject focus could be reinforcing topic work. The process of moving spaces forward/backward and perhaps multiplying the dice number is arithmetical. In addition, the activities involve problem solving, creativity and use of language. With this range of links to other curriculum areas, it is easy to see how creating algorithms and computational thinking can be cross-curricular and embedded into good primary school practice. The ideas outlined lend themselves to personalising the learning both in computer science and in other curriculum areas.

Assessment

The lesson outlined included peer and self-assessment as a key part of the process. Peer assessment helps the assessor to clarify his or her thinking, as well as enhance the understanding of the assessed child. Self-assessment further extends many of the benefits of peer assessment and encourages pupils to see the connection between what they have done and the lesson objective, and encourages ownership of their own learning (Black and Williams, 1990).

The lesson idea used small whiteboards for self-assessment. Although not foolproof, it gives the teacher an insight into the pupils' understanding, which again helps with the continuous cycle of planning lessons based on assessment information gained while teaching.

A useful way to assess pupil understanding and identify the next steps for learning might be to incorporate an 'I can' assessment, as below:

- I can make an algorithm with a purpose.

- I can edit my algorithm to improve it.

- I can explain why I have included certain features within my algorithm.

- I can evaluate other algorithms and explain how they could be improved.

In addition to peer and self-assessment, adult observation, including using digital cameras to record the algorithms created, will provide the teacher with key information on the pupils' understanding, which is vital when planning future sessions. Audio recordings may also provide some rich information relating to the pupils' attainment and thinking. Tablet computers are another means for either structured or unstructured recording of pupils working or reflecting on what they have learnt.

The lesson outlined is of a social constructivist nature and follows the ideas of Vygotsky (1978) in that the learning is based around the collaboration of others, rather than any independent achievement. Although the pupils are constructing meaning from the tasks suggested, the lesson is based on the potential achievement of the child through the zone of proximal development (ZPD) and collaboration with others. The ZPD differs in size between individuals; the key is to remember that each child has the potential to achieve more with guidance from an adult or in discussion with a peer, especially if the peer is more capable.

Reflective questions

1. Consider how you can embed the understanding of algorithms into your current teaching while not losing sight of the Programme of Study for Computing (DfE, 2013): *understand what algorithms are and how they are implemented on digital devices; and that programs execute by following precise and unambiguous instructions.*

2. How can you encourage the use of the correct terminology?

3. How would you respond to parents who tell you their child is not old enough to learn about computing and the associated terminology?

Summary

It is worth reflecting that this first chapter, which outlines the teaching of computer science and, more specifically, algorithms in KS1, has been almost entirely based on using non-digital resources, sometimes referred to as 'unplugged' learning. In this lesson the use of digital technology relates more to assessment than the main activities. It is important to keep this idea in mind, because although ultimately the concepts should lead to the creation of ideas using digital devices, the fundamental processes are very often best understood using non-digital activities.

Although the idea of teaching computing to pupils in KS1 may seem new, the teaching pedagogy these ideas are based on is well tested and researched and seen as good practice within a KS1 setting. The ideas are practical and cross-curricular and should be related to the pupils' interest and prior experience. It is vital to see this as being embedded into current practice and not a bolt-on; this helps with continuity and progression and gives the lessons relevance. It is important to note how the learning can be personalised and the role of self- and peer assessment.

Having outlined the cross-curricular gains, do not lose sight of the computing aspect. The pupils need to understand what the term algorithm means and the relevance to digital devices, which need clear and unambiguous instructions, having been decomposed into a sequence of simpler steps.

The focus of this chapter is on understanding algorithms but this must not be seen in isolation – it is an early step in the whole process of computational thinking. The next chapter considers ways to teach programming at KS1, which is a natural progression, as all programs are based on an algorithmic process.

Useful links

http://barefootcas.org.uk/activities

An excellent range of teaching activities.

http://barefootcas.org.uk/sample-resources/algorithms

Valuable resources for teachers.

http://code-it.co.uk

Many computer science resources and ideas.

http://code-it.co.uk/unplugged/writesandwichalgorithm2.pdf

Making a sandwich game.

www.iboard.co.uk/teacher/jlisaw8/1

KS1 sequencing games.

Further reading

Bagge, P (2015) *How to Teach Primary Programming Using Scratch: Teacher's Handbook (Code-IT Primary Programming).* Buckingham: University of Buckingham Press.

Berry, M (2013) *Computing in the National Curriculum: A Guide for Primary Teachers.* Available online at: www.computingatschool.org.uk/primary (accessed 20 December 2016).

Harrison, J (2013) *Guidance for Primary Teachers.* Naace. Available online at: www.computingatschool. org.uk/data/uploads/CASPrimaryComputing.pdf (accessed 20 December 2016).

An excellent guide to the philosophy behind computing in the primary school, with a very good section on KS1.

Melmoth, J, Dickins, LS and Nielsen, S (2015) *Coding for Beginners.* Wolverhampton: Usborne Publishing.

References

Black, P and Williams, D (1990) *Inside the Black Box.* London: King's College.

CAS (2012) *Computer Science: A Curriculum for Schools.* London: Computing At School.

Collins, W (2011) *The New Collins Concise English Dictionary.* Glasgow: HarperCollins.

Curzon, P (1999) *Learning Computers through Games and Puzzles.* Middlesex: Middlesex University.

DfE (2013) *The National Curriculum for England and Wales.* London: DfE.

Vygotsky, L (1978) *Interactions between Learning and Development from Mind and Society.* Cambridge, MA: Harvard University Press.

Chapter 2

Programming in KS1

analyse problems in computational forms

Learning outcomes

This chapter looks at how to develop the pupils' understanding of writing and debugging simple computer programs, using logical reasoning to predict the behaviour of these programs.

By the end of this chapter you should be able to:

- engage the children in being able to write, execute and debug simple computer programs;
- facilitate children in exploring the principles of computer programming;
- enable children to predict the behaviour of simple programs.

Teachers' Standards

Working through this chapter will help you meet the following standards:

3a. Have a secure knowledge of the relevant subject(s) and curriculum areas, foster and maintain pupils' interest in the subject and address misunderstandings.
4b. Promote the love of learning and pupils' intellectual curiosity.

Links to the National Curriculum

Pupils should learn to:

- create and debug simple programs;
- use logical reasoning to predict the behaviour of simple programs.

Introduction

This chapter will build upon exploring algorithms, described in Chapter 1, and make the transition from unplugged activities such as role play to writing sequences of instructions to control robots, leading to onscreen programming.

As with Chapter 1, the focus is on meeting the statutory requirement in a manner which professionals would consider manageable, appropriate for the age range and embedded in good practice. This can again be achieved without the need for 'expert' knowledge.

The key difference between writing an algorithm, as discussed in Chapter 1, and writing a computer program is the need to present information in a manner a computer can understand – in other words, a computer programming language. There are a variety of programming languages, each with its own vocabulary and grammar. The computer language or code is then interpreted into machine code, which the computer uses to operate.

Programming at Key Stage 1 (KS1) is not, however, about understanding complex code! We will start by inventing our own code, so children understand the principles, before moving on to programming instructions and finally to age-appropriate programming languages.

Lesson idea: programming a friend!

This lesson focus is on how to develop further the understanding gained in Chapter 1 on algorithms, so the children experience writing a simple computer program in a very practical manner.

Before you start

The children will need to have some understanding that computer programs are based on algorithms (see Chapter 1) and therefore need precise instructions.

They will need to be in groups of three.

Things you need

This lesson works best if it takes place in a large hall or playground with an obstacle course set up (so far it may sound like a PE lesson!).

You need:

- one beanbag for each group of pupils;
- a board/flip chart.

Context

First, it is important that the children are encouraged to use the correct language. They also need to be aware that, when programming or writing code, not only does the sequence of instructions (algorithm) need to be decomposed into a lot of small steps but specific commands are also needed.

In this lesson, the children are going to experience programming a human robot friend using specific commands and relate this to the appropriate terminology.

Learning objectives

- To be able to write a simple program using appropriate commands.
- To be able to debug the program and predict the logical outcomes.

Lesson outline

Class introduction

The pupils assemble in the hall or playground. The teacher outlines the objectives of the lesson and sets clear ground rules on the expectations and also emphasises safety issues.

The teacher demonstrates with a pupil, who follows the precise commands given: left foot forward, right foot forward, stop, turn. This will include recording the code.

Commentary

It is worth considering whether to engage the pupils in inventing all or some of the commands. This will depend on the class and the time available. There are many advantages in deciding the language with the children, as it will engage them more fully with the idea of using computer code.

Appropriate commands could be as shown in Figure 2.1.

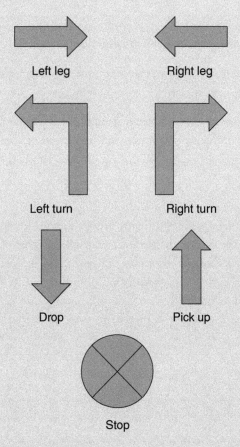

Figure 2.1 Possible symbols for commands

It is important to agree symbols for each of the commands, so that the programmer does not need to keep writing everything in long hand.

Commentary

At this stage the name given to each command is not as important as the pupils knowing that the commands are the only instruction the human robot will understand. They also need to be clear that they are going to create the algorithm (sequence of instructions) for the robot to follow.

Classroom organisation

Ideally there will be enough space for the children to work in threes, but bear in mind that if space is restricted, a larger group may be necessary. Two of the three pupils will be responsible for writing the program and the third will play the robot. A group of three works well as it enables the programmers to discuss the program and therefore gain from each other's ideas. It also means that, from a practical point of view, the children have more space for each robot than if they were in pairs.

All that is needed is a bench, a table and a beanbag, but this can of course differ according to resources and the teacher's imagination!

The programmers need to write down the program. Writing it on an A4 whiteboard is ideal, as the program can then easily be edited (debugged).

Each time the programmers have written a section of the program, they need to give the instructions to the human robot to execute. It is best to encourage the pupils to test a small part of the program first. Regularly ask the pupils to change roles so all children have a chance to be both programmer and robot.

It will not be long before the children will start thinking about the parameters, e.g. what distance is meant by a step? This helps bring in accuracy but it is probably best that the children discover this by themselves, so it will be more meaningful to them. Pupils are also likely to ask about repetition. They may wish to write 'repeat next' to an instruction a number of times. This would save time and lead to the program running more efficiently. If they ask a child to do something more than once, they will naturally discover repeated loops. The coding is becoming more precise and more efficient.

Commentary

This whole process is fully immersing the pupils into a programming experience: they will naturally make logical predictions of how the program will behave. In their desire to succeed they will constantly be reviewing the program and debugging it.

Throughout this process the teacher has a key role in guiding and facilitating the pupils' understanding of programming procedures, without taking the process over.

Mini-plenary

It will be valuable to stop the children at some point. This would be an ideal time for a short demonstration by a group and a discussion on any problems found but, more importantly, solutions. The pupils will naturally be debugging their computer code. It may well be that pupils have discovered ways to speed the process of programming up by using a repetition of commands. The children may learn from each other here.

Differentiation

This activity would lend itself to being in mixed-ability groups, with the less able pupils gaining from the support of the more able. It is likely that some children will have excellent programming ideas but be less able at recording them; working with a child who can record the idea more easily would be beneficial.

If a group completes the task within the time allocated, the activity could be extended by making the obstacle course longer or more difficult. This may mean that the pupils need to develop their computer code further.

Assessment

An audio or video recording of the execution of the program would be an excellent record of achievement. Remember, it is the process that is important and not just the final outcome. A quick video clip of the discussion on an iPad may reveal a great deal. This could then be used with the whole class at some stage to reinforce and celebrate the programmers' achievements.

Plenary

Ask the children to work with a different group to test the program. A pupil could be given the task of recording this for assessment purposes. If through assessment for learning you discover the children have mastered the task, an extension would be for them to look at the written symbols and predict what will happen.

The teacher should reinforce the key vocabulary: execute, decompose, repetition, debug.

Activity

What computing concepts has this lesson immersed the children in? Can you think of a way you could develop these concepts further?

Taking it further

The next stages of writing, executing and debugging a program would be to use a programmable toy, such as a Bee-Bot.

Bee-Bots are very simple for children to operate, as they have just four directional commands: forward, backward and right-angle turns.

If we keep in mind that writing a computer program or code is a set of specific instructions for a predetermined outcome, then directing a Bee-Bot to a given destination is doing just that.

One approach would be to use a mat designed for a Bee-Bot and ask the children to program the Bee-Bot to move from one place on the mat to another. If desired, the children could build the route themselves using Lego or other appropriate items and follow the path they have created. These simple tasks involve a whole host of computational skills. Like most programmers the pupils are unlikely to create a program that works perfectly first time, so they are likely to need to debug the program. The children should be encouraged to identify any fault and then follow a logical process to fix it and retest the program. Working in pairs is really good for this, as it encourages discussion and a shared approach to problem solving. If the level of challenge is appropriate, the children are likely to make errors in the original program but should have the capability to debug it themselves. As a teacher, it is important to facilitate the discussion relating to debugging but not to provide the solutions. It is through this that children are learning key skills in writing and debugging code, while developing the associated skills of problem solving, independent working and resilience. They will learn a great deal more by finding their own solutions, coupled with a significantly increased sense of satisfaction with a successfully completed program. Using video for assessment purposes would again work really well.

In the early stages pupils will endeavour to program a Bee-Bot by trial and error but we should move on from this and encourage them to predict the outcome. By writing the commands in short hand, e.g. FD 1, RT 90, FD 2, etc., the children are writing the code for the program and predicting the behaviour of a simple program. FD 1 is a logical programming short hand: it is starting the children on the path of recognising the code used in the Logo programming language, which they may meet in KS2. Using RT 90 and LT 90 is again a step to writing the code for Logo, although less obvious. A Bee-Bot right-angle turn is just a turn symbol. This may be appropriate but it is worth considering preparing them for the next step in programming.

An alternative to the children writing the programming commands could be to put the commands on cards and for the children to move them into the correct place. This makes debugging easier, as it keeps the focus on computing skills rather than writing. There will be some children who have an excellent understanding of how to program a robot but who may struggle with literacy. Unlike the children we teach, computers are completely predictable! Once we understand the commands, we know exactly how they will behave. We should encourage the children to understand this predictability, using logical reasoning to predict the behaviour of simple programs.

An extension might be to give the children a set of code for programming a Bee-Bot with errors built in. The children would have to debug the program. This has several benefits as it reinforces the predictability of a program, whilst strengthening the understanding that debugging programs is part of the process of writing code.

This can be further developed by writing the code onscreen, using Bee-Bot PC software or the Bee-Bot app. The process of writing a program and debugging is similar to the initial idea of using an actual Bee-Bot, but the children have made a step from the physical world to onscreen programming. This is an important step in the process of understanding computer programming. It is also possible to control a Bee-Bot through a series of 12 levels of an ancient Egyptian pyramid, using Bee-Bot Pyramid. This Bee-Bot app teaches children how to direct and move their Bee-Bot character by giving it a set of sequential commands.

If you wish the children to explore directional arrows as an early step to programming, the TES iboard has some useful activities: **www.iboard.co.uk/teacher/jlisaw8/2**.

Further programming skills could be developed using more advanced floor robots such as a Pro-Bot, which would appeal to many children. This is a car that will accept programming commands using arrow keys but will also accept more complex commands, meeting the needs of the more able.

A logical step after working with an onscreen Bee-Bot might be 2Go (part of the Purple Mash suite of programs).

2Go enables children to direct an onscreen robot around the screen. This can either be to a set destination or it may just leave a trail indicating where it has moved. It is programmed by entering commands, using arrow keys and a numeric keypad. It starts off being very straightforward but it provides an increasing challenge, enabling the more able children to simulate a range of environments. As they write the code the children will naturally discuss their programs, modifying, debugging and improving their algorithm.

We have so far achieved a progression from programming a friend, working with a programmable object to onscreen environments which in turn have led to slightly more sophisticated angles of turn and backgrounds. The process is moving ever closer to a more abstract approach of inputting code. This will be explored more fully when we discuss programming at KS2. The stages of progression are set out in such a manner that the process of programming becomes increasingly intuitive to the children.

If, by the end of KS1, the majority of the children can comfortably use an onscreen version of a program like 2Go, they will be well placed to meet the demands of programming at KS2.

As children become increasingly exposed to programming, the level of attainment will rise, so we must be vigilant in making sure that we provide the correct level of challenge. A simplified version of Seymour Papert's (1993) Logo programming language, such as 2Logo, is a very suitable first step into more complex forms of code. It provides a user-friendly screen and easy access to the common Logo programming commands, leading children to input code to create regular polygons, using repeat commands, and then to name a procedure.

There are an ever-increasing number of apps and programs being developed to meet the need for children to program at KS1. It is important to keep in mind how the program is developing the children's understanding of the concepts and the terms of computing. In addition, consider the extent to which it provides a wealth of creative and open-ended activities.

ScratchJr is a brilliant free app, which is an easier version of the much-acclaimed graphical programming software called Scratch. We shall explore how Scratch might be used in Chapter 4. Scratch was initially invented to teach children as young as eight how to program using graphical blocks instead of text, and ScratchJr aims to engage children in onscreen programming at a much younger age. ScratchJr consists of simple directional and control blocks, which are slotted together to make a sprite move.

Hopscotch is a free app that facilitates the user making games as well as playing them. The emphasis is on the children having fun with its colourful, friendly interface. There are plenty of helpful tutorials, enabling the building of all kinds of apps whilst learning the principles of programming.

Rapid Router (**www.codeforlife.education/rapidrouter/3**) is a free web-based teaching resource for Key Stage 1 and lower Key Stage 2, which teaches the children the basic principles of programming through a coding game which is differentiated by levels. It uses the visual programming technique. The programme enables teachers to monitor and manage individual progress.

J2Code (**www.j2e.com/j2code**) provides an excellent range of opportunities for coding in the primary school. This again is free and has the advantage that it can be used on any platform without logins. J2Code includes JIT for KS1, a graphical programming language and a text-based language. All programs include free lesson plans and examples to explore. In this chapter we will consider JIT, which allows the user to control a sprite by simple directional arrows. Although it can be operated without needing to use text, any sprite movement is recorded on the side of the screen, which can be reordered if the child wants to edit their program. There are two levels: simple, where the sprite responds straight away, and advanced, where the code via the directional arrows is stored until play is activated.

Another valuable tool is Daisy the Dinosaur, by Hopscotch Technologies. The children are shown how to program the dinosaur to move, jump, grow and shrink. The children can design their own programs for Daisy using this free app. It involves the processes of writing, executing and debugging a program in a very child-friendly way.

There are further activities and games that can be created in 2DIY. These can be from matching activities through to platform games. Children are able to create an activity or platform game in an easily accessible manner. This is without the need for them to write complex code but still embracing the concepts of programming. As with other programs children can edit and debug, adding repetitive loops within their programs.

If you wish to challenge the children further, the Kodable app may be appropriate. The context is very much at KS1 level, where children are helping the 'fuzzFamily' solve problems in the planet's 'Technomaze'. The 'fuzzFamily' are very logical and follow every command exactly as they are told. This is developing the skills of writing algorithms within a program but it takes the pupils' understanding a step further, with the opportunity to use conditional statements like 'If this, then that', in addition to using repeat commands in loops. There are also opportunities within Kodable to debug and use critical thinking, not only to solve problems but also to predict the program outcome. This encourages children to deal with potential bugs before they occur.

Discussion

The key focus of this chapter, and the associated lesson ideas, has been related to programming and the importance of using logical reasoning to predict the behaviour of simple programs.

By learning to program in an age-appropriate way, the pupils are developing a rich understanding of the world around them, and are also developing many transferable skills.

Beyond the long-term desire for young people to develop knowledge and understanding and to be innovative in the world of computer science, children should also have some understanding of the world around them. The digital world does not work by magic! By providing them with meaningful, open-ended tasks the children will learn how to construct their own meaning, develop a degree of independence and perseverance, and acquire many problem-solving skills. Making learning meaningful and purposeful is a vital ingredient in inspiring children to learn.

For many teachers, a recurring theme will be the unfamiliarity of exposing very young children to the concepts of programming. Although the ideas outlined are appropriate for KS1, there will be concerns as to how children may cope.

Michalakis (2012), alias Dr Techniko, has run sessions for children in which they program their parents by giving them a code to move. He has noted a pattern in children mastering the concepts of computing through having fun with programming and has concluded that, when children have fun, they become increasingly smart and creative about programming.

A pilot study in Massachusetts (Flannery *et al.*, 2013) researched into the impact of children between the ages of four and seven during the development stage of ScratchJr. In the pilot study the children were gradually introduced to the concepts, which became more complex as the child progressed. On just their third day with ScratchJr, the children were introduced to the idea of programming tasks in parallel. They were asked to make a snake wriggle across a grassy field whilst at the same time a bird glided down from the air. This involved two separate strings of commands, one controlling the bird and the other the snake, and the commands needed to work simultaneously. The children were able to master this and some added a repetition loop, so the snake was able to slither through the grass again and again. Some went further and controlled exactly when the snake glided down in relation to the bird. In computing terms this is control flow, a key computer programming concept. Pupils would not think of this as programming loops or control flow, but that does not matter. At a very young age, they have started to understand the computer programming process in a fun and engaging manner, developing a broad range of skills, which is much more than just the computer science focus. Being able to think like this can help children in maths and science, even in learning to write, which all require children to be able to organise their thoughts into the best order. The children in the Massachusetts study, who were only aged between four and seven, embraced the tasks very well and naturally understood concepts that could be defined as computer programming. The pilot study not only demonstrated children's capabilities to program in KS1 but also that the children loved the open-ended creative nature of the activities, which develop a broad range of skills, not just programming. Bers, cited in Guernsey (2013), calls programming *a language of expression*, making it a natural fit for the Early Years, when children are learning how to express themselves.

Early exposure to programming seems to have helped some of the world's top coders. Google engineer Neil Fraser, cited in Reilly (2013), surveyed over 100 of his co-workers about when they first picked up coding, and then compared that with their performance on a simple test of skills. He found that those who wrote their first code between the ages of roughly 8 and 11 were most likely to develop advanced coding skills. This survey is not very robust in research terms and is taken from a narrow band of people, but it did indicate a pattern. This may not be surprising but the issue has also been that only a small minority of children would have been exposed to any writing of code at a young age. The software is now there to enable children to develop programming skills at an even younger age. Providing the opportunity for all children to write code at KS1 means that all children have the opportunity to realise their potential. It may also mean that the pupils with the greatest aptitude for programming will be developing advanced code in adulthood and not just the individuals who have been given the opportunity by chance.

Ray Kurzell, cited in Bridges (2012), believes learning how to program is going to be the most useful new skill we can teach our children today. Our lives increasingly depend on how good we are at instructing computers. They hold our personal data and they are often an integral part of the decision-making process. Kurzell believes that if we do not learn programming as children, we will never evolve. He also argues that *the only second language you should worry about your kids learning is programming.* These views are open to debate but we should all recognise the importance of all children having some understanding of the process of computer programming in this digital age.

Activity

Outline the skills children would develop in the lesson example. Consider whether you should teach programming in a discrete or embedded manner.

Reflective questions

- To what extent are the skills of computer programming at KS1 transferable to other aspects of learning?

- What do you understand to be the key points of progression for computer programming at KS1?

- Computer programming is a 'language of expression'. Do you agree?

Summary

This chapter outlines how children can move from computer programming, with an unplugged learning approach, to develop the skills needed to program onscreen. The pupils would have all used key terms such as algorithms, sequence, repetition, debug and code. Some may have gone further and used conditional statements such as, 'If this, then that'.

The chapter has considered how the very specific skills of programming can support the children's learning across the curriculum. The activities outlined will also help with developing perseverance, problem solving and the use of logic.

The chapter considers how, given the opportunity, children can engage with programming activities at a young age in a manner which is appropriate to their learning. Computer programming provides opportunities for success for all children and wonderful challenges for the most able.

Useful links

www.iboard.co.uk/teacher/jlisaw8/2

Some very good directional activities.

www.codeforlife.education/rapidrouter/3

www.j2e.com/j2code

www.youtube.com/watch?v=1XxKHHdNEA4

A good introduction to using Bee-Bots.

www.youtube.com/watch?v=YbP-9pSf9Ng&feature=player_embedded

The Animal Project preschool programming by the DevTech Research Group (2012).

Children programming devices at a young age.

Further reading

Bagge, P (2015) *How to Teach Primary Programming Using Scratch: Teacher's Handbook (Code-IT Primary Programming)*. Buckingham: University of Buckingham Press.

Berry, M (2013) *Computing in the National Curriculum: A Guide for Primary Teachers*. Available online at: www.computingatschool.org.uk/primary (accessed 20 December 2016).

Bridges, D (2012) *Children and Computing*. Available at: www.inpractice.org (accessed 20 December 2016).

Chapman, H (2012) *Introducing Programming to Preschoolers*. Waltham, MA: MindShift.

Melmoth, J, Dickins, R and Nielsen, S (2015) *Coding for Beginners*. Wolverhampton: Usborne Publishing.

References

Flannery, LP, Kazakoff, ER, Bontá, P, Silverman, B, Bers, MU and Resnick, M (2013) Designing ScratchJr: support for early childhood learning through computer programming. In: *Proceedings of the 12th International Conference on Interaction Design and Children* (IDC '13). New York: ACM, pp1–10.

Guernsey, L (2013) Very young programmers. In: *New York Times*, education edition. Available online at: www.nytimes.com/2013/09/03/science/very-young-programmers.html?_r=1& (accessed 20 December 2016).

Michalakis, N (2012) How to train your robot. Available online at: http://drtechniko.com/2012/04/09/how-to-train-your-robot (accessed 20 December 2016).

Papert, S (1993) *Mindstorms: Children, Computers, and Powerful Ideas*, 2nd edn. New York: Basic Books.

Reilly, M (2013) Kindergarten coders can program before they can read. Available online at: www.newscientist.com/.../mg21929275-800-kindergarten-coders-can-program (accessed 20 December 2016).

Chapter 3

Manipulating digital content in KS1

become digitally literate

Learning outcomes

By the end of this chapter you should be able to:

- develop an understanding of ways of creating opportunities for children to manipulate digital content;
- design a series of lessons which allow creation and editing of digital content within a range of subjects;
- understand approaches to teaching and learning which enable children to explore their own methods of manipulating digital content.

Teachers' Standards

Working through this chapter will help you meet the following standards:

3a. Have a secure knowledge of the relevant subject(s) and curriculum areas, foster and maintain pupils' interest in the subject, and address misunderstandings.

4a. Impart knowledge and develop understanding through effective use of lesson time.

4b. Promote a love of learning and children's intellectual curiosity.

6a. Know and understand how to assess the relevant subject and curriculum areas, including statutory assessment requirements.

Links to the National Curriculum

National Curriculum 2014, Computing Programme of Study, KS1 Subject Content

Pupils should learn to:

- use technology purposefully to create, organise, store, manipulate and retrieve digital content.

Introduction

This chapter will consider opportunities for Key Stage 1 (KS1) children to manipulate digital content. The lesson idea will look at how video, sound or images can be used in a creative way. This will be related to the personal experiences of KS1 children. Further discussion will consider ways to help young children to see themselves as information gatherers and creative producers.

Lesson idea

The sequence of lessons outlined below is an engaging way of using digital technology to achieve creative outcomes in a thematic way. The lessons are intended to be used with children in either Years 1 or 2 and could be delivered as a block of lessons over one or two days or as a series of lessons over a number of weeks. The intention is to embed opportunities to create and manipulate digital content in a thematic way, ideally as part of an existing topic or theme that the class is following. This type of approach works best when children have opportunities to compare and contrast being digitally creative with being creative with other types of non-digital media.

This sequence of lessons carefully ensures that children develop a range of skills in a sequential manner. They will learn with a blend of non-digital and digital tools and approaches – this allows teachers to design delivery to allow effective support for use of digital resources.

Things you need

- Tablets or computers – the amount will depend on how the lessons are designed. This sequence of lessons allowed the class to work in two groups supported by the class teacher, teaching assistant and digital leaders. Half the class worked with the teaching assistant – therefore only seven laptops were needed.

- Audio-editing software – these lessons use a free editor called Audacity, available at **http://audacity.sourceforge.net**. You could use other online tools, such as Creaza AudioEditor (**www.creazaeducation.com/this-is-creaza/AudioEditor**) or there is a range of tablet apps, such as Recordium (**http://recordiumapp.com**).

- Audacity tutorial: **http://audacity.sourceforge.net/manual-1.2/tutorials.html**.

- Microphones – either external or integral to a computer or tablet.

- Access to a range of online audio files.

This lesson sequence focused on a painting called *La Nuit* by Vernet, which you can find at: **www.nationalgallery.org.uk/initial-teacher-education/primary/learning/vernet.aspx**.

Before you start

It would be useful for children to have time to familiarise themselves with the audio-editing software that you choose to use. These lessons used Audacity. Before these lessons, children had time working with Audacity to record their own voices and to experiment with some of the editing tools.

Context

As with lessons discussed in other chapters it is important to ensure that the children have a purpose and 'real' context for their work with digital media. This sequence of lessons is completely embedded within a thematic approach to the curriculum. The lessons were part of a wider theme using methods developed within the National Gallery's Take One Picture approach to curriculum development (**www. takeonepicture.org**).

Learning objectives

- Develop skills in recording, editing and manipulating digital audio files.

- Be able to justify choices for the design of digital media.

- Portray images using digital media.

Lesson outline

This describes a series of lessons aimed at creating 'soundscapes' to portray a scene from a painting that was studied as part of a Take One Picture project. The children had already undertaken a number of pieces of work and projects focused on developing understanding and focus on this painting. For instance, they had written a number of fiction and non-fiction pieces, such as a description of a part of the painting, instructions for the fishermen and a story about 'wreckers' and smugglers. The children had designed and made ships as part of a design and technology project, which also brought in development of historical skills, looking at artefacts and items from other ages. In music the children had listened to, discussed and performed sea shanties and other maritime-themed songs.

This sequence of lessons was delivered across a morning on one day per week for four weeks. The class teacher was working for one day per week in this Year 1/2 class. Overall, English, music and ICT were the main subjects being developed during the sessions.

Session 1

The first session started by discussing some of the work they had already completed, which had focused on *La Nuit*. This allowed children to recap what they already knew about the painting and what questions they still had about what was going on in different areas. The class teacher then focused the children on one specific area – the fireside scene.

The class then had some time to look in more detail at the fire scene, using the zoomable digital image of *La Nuit* available at **www.nationalgallery.org.uk/initial-teacher-education/primary/learning/zoom_vernet.html**. The children, using laptops, were able to explore the digital image themselves. This then led to a discussion and some work describing the scene using a range of rich vocabulary – this was related to work looking at descriptive writing in English that the children had been following during the week.

During this sequence of lessons the class was fortunate to have teaching assistant support all of the time. The school had also developed a system of using digital leaders. Digital leaders were a number of Year 6 pupils who had taken on the role of developing digital skills with pupils and staff. As a group they met one lunchtime per week and received training on a core range of tools and skills that could be used to support learning across the school.

After their descriptive writing work, half of the class then looked at what type of sounds they thought they might hear if they were in the fire scene of *La Nuit*. This discussion, built on a number of other music sessions, developed children's skills looking at how instruments can be played in different ways to make different sounds.

At the end of this discussion the teacher started to discuss how sounds could be recorded using digital devices. During the year the children had already had some experience in recording their voices using Talk Time cards and talking tins and using Audacity as a whole class.

At the same time as this music session, the teaching assistant began introducing children to Audacity. Audacity is a free, multitrack audio editor that can be downloaded and used on Windows, Apple, Linux and other operating systems (**http://audacity.sourceforge.net**).

The children were already familiar with this software as the teacher has used this with the whole class to record and play back some of their ideas within other English sessions. During this session the children had the opportunity, in pairs using laptops and external microphones, to record and play back their own voices. They began to record their voices using different 'tracks' and they also recorded different sounds to accompany their voices. The teaching assistant then introduced the children to ways of editing, clipping and balancing sound using some of the tools within Audacity.

After they had completed these tasks the groups swapped and worked on the other activity. Following this the class then came back together and the class teacher focused discussion on one particular part of the fire scene, the old man leaning on a barrel. The class teacher carefully steered around to a discussion where the children decided that the old man might have been telling some type of story. The class started thinking about what type of story he could be telling. The class then read some pirate and sea stories.

Session 2

The class teacher introduced the class to the idea of soundscapes. The class then listened to a number of soundscapes: **http://sounds.bl.uk/environment/soundscapes** or **https://soundcloud.com/groups/soundscapes** have good examples. (The examples were carefully chosen to ensure that they were appropriate for use in a primary classroom.)

Discussion then moved on to how the class could create soundscapes using a range of percussion instruments and voice. The children then had the opportunity to create their own short soundscapes in pairs, which they recorded using talking tins. These were then played back to the whole class, followed by discussion of what the sounds were meant to portray.

Commentary

During discussion of digital work like this it is important to give adequate time for children to evaluate their own and others' work.

The class then began to tell their stories. A first step was to decide in pairs what they thought the story was about. Here are some of their story ideas:

- a little girl and a crab;

- a pirate captain and a parrot;

- a magic shark and a man;

- a pirate finds a parrot.

The children then went on to plan and write the first part of their stories. As with the previous week, this built on work the children had focused on in English lessons during the week. The children decided on an overall structure for their story, identified some of the key words and 'exciting' vocabulary and then began to write the first sections of the story. The class teacher developed this work with half of the class.

The teaching assistant then took the other half of the class to work with Audacity. The focus of this session was to start importing a range of sounds that the class had identified could be heard around the fire scene in the painting. The children were shown a range of websites where sounds and sound clips are stored (**www. soundboard.com** and **www.freesound.org** are good examples). The class teacher had already downloaded a number of sounds, such as flickering flames, waves, bells and horse hooves, in a folder on the network. The children were then able to learn how to import sound files into different tracks within Audacity and then use their skills in copying, pasting and cropping to manipulate the sounds.

Session 3

In the third session the English lesson objective was to develop and redraft stories. Each pair discussed their existing stories, made some notes about what they could add or develop and then came for a short discussion with the class teacher or teaching assistant. This allowed a discussion based on marking and feedback from the previous week's work and focus on what they could do to improve their stories. Part of this discussion centred on the careful use of vocabulary to portray the scene they were trying to recreate. Following their 'tutorial' the children went on to write a final draft of their stories.

After a little proofreading and editing, the class, in pairs, practised reading their stories aloud to each other. At the same time the teaching assistant started to record their stories, using an external microphone and laptop, straight into Audacity. This was an important part of the process – the children had an opportunity to record, review and rerecord their stories. The teaching assistant carefully created a master copy of their recorded story in a network folder. The children then had an opportunity to go and develop their stories using some of the tools they had learnt previously. The whole class then reviewed the recordings – again, practising some of their evaluation and review skills.

Session 4

The final session allowed the children in their pairs to work on developing their overall soundscapes. They had the opportunity to review their stories. If they felt that they would like to make changes, by rerecording a part or all of their stories, they made 'appointments' with the teaching assistant – however, they had to provide a justification of why their changes would make the story recording better.

At the same time the children started to finalise the sound effects they would use alongside their stories to create the soundscape. During the morning the class teacher downloaded and made available any extra sound effects that the children required – some extra sounds had also been downloaded during the week. The children downloaded and imported sounds into their Audacity file. They then cut, sliced, rebalanced and generally edited their soundscape 'tracks' to create the effect they desired. During this session digital leaders were used to work with the children. This gave the opportunity for much more adult or older 'reponsible' child input into developing the soundscapes.

At the end of the morning the class had an opportunity to share their finished soundscapes with the whole class. There was considerable discussion about what they thought they had learnt during the whole process. There was also some initial discussion about what they thought they could improve.

Taking it further

An ideal way of extending these ideas further for KS1 children is to think of a range of ways in which we can create digital outcomes/artefacts. This lesson idea focused on producing digital audio files; another approach would be to create digital videos. Later we point to discussions of the way in which certain modes of communication may have an impact on the way children will form their ideas and understanding. Certainly this project works well with an audio file linked to a static image/painting. However, it would also be interesting to produce a role play of the same scene using video – this would change the nature of what the children were trying to achieve but could be equally as valid as a way of showing reflection about the painting in focus.

Digital storytelling tools could also be used by children of this age. Online tools such as Storybird, Little Bird Tales, Kerpoof or purchased software such as 2Simple's 2Create a Story will all allow children to create digital stories. Some of these could be ideal to provide an alternative means of portraying the scene and achieve similar outcomes to this lesson. When using digital storytelling tools it is interesting to note the different ways in which they allow children to combine images, drawings and text. Some tools restrict children to a set of images and then allow text to be added. Other tools allow choice and/or drawings of images to be combined with text.

Discussion

Building information-enabled classrooms

In the last few years there has developed a widespread recognition that good teaching should also include the appropriate use of technology. Current learning-focused judgements of classroom practice also indicate a desire to use a range of technological tools that impact on learning. Indeed, recent advice about lesson observations to Ofsted inspectors from Her Majesty's Chief Inspector Michael Wilshaw included a reference to the use of technology to support learning (a reference is made to the letter in TES, 2014).

McGregor (2007) discusses the many features and theories of learning, which include a number of references to 'construction' and 'processing' of knowledge. We could then accept that knowledge is the way in which we piece 'fragments' of information together. Therefore, for learning to be successful, teachers need to have some considered focus on the ways in which they 'draw in' and 'process' information in their classrooms. Access to a wider variety of information using a range of modes of communication seems essential to allow children to form knowledge, which should then lead to learning.

When thinking about our primary classrooms it may be useful to develop a model analogous to computational theories of mind or perhaps information-processing approaches within psychology (Horst, 1996; Buckler and Castle, 2013). A pedagogical model of this nature could suggest a 'flow' of information in our classrooms. The terms 'inputs', 'processes' and 'outcomes' could then be used to signify the processes within this 'flow'. A model of this nature is then usefully employed to create some order and structure to the large range of web and social media tools that could be used in schools. Table 3.1 provides some examples of how different tools could be included within this pedagogical model (it gives indicative examples; further examples can be found at **http://goo.gl/fIdGRC**). These are mainly online tools which can be accessed via a range of devices, including tablet computers. We have not included a full range of tablet apps within this chapter – these are included in Chapter 8.

Table 3.1 Examples of useful tools within a pedagogical model

Stages in the process	Groupings of tools	Examples of tools
Inputs	Web searching	Google
		Bing
		Yahoo
		Swiggle
		Kidrex
	Video	British Pathé
		TeacherTube
		SnagFilms
	Sound	SoundCloud
		FindSounds
		Soundboard
	Images	Creative Commons
		Arkive
		Sprixi
	Activities	National Education Network (NEN)
		ShowMe
		National Geographic
Processes	Gathering and collaborating	Padlet
		Linoit
		Wikispaces
	Organising and storing	Delicious
		3x3Links
		Popplet
	Reflecting	Padlet
		VoiceThread
		Blog posts and comments

Outcomes	Audio, video and animation	Audacity
		MS Movie Maker
		Super Action Comic Maker (culturestreet.org.uk)
	Annotate photos and images	Animoto
		PhotoPeach
		MS Photo Story
	Digital storytelling	Storybird
		ZooBurst
		Little Bird Tales

On a daily basis, information 'flows' into, through and out of our classrooms. We ask children to bring in information and we source information from a range of non-digital sources. However, teachers also need to build their own 'banks' of digital information sources. Table 3.1 gives us some idea of a basic way of thinking about structuring the many resources that are available. When we plan any unit of work it is useful to think of how we are going to source information – do we have a stock of images, sounds or video that we can go back to? Do we then provide children with adequate opportunity to reflect and organise their ideas? Do we also then allow children to use a range of ways of combining information and knowledge to show their learning?

Accessing digital information and allowing children to manipulate this into creative ways of presenting ideas is an approach that may take time to develop.

Assessing digital learning

Another area to consider is how we assess the processes and products of children's digital work. The current Primary National Curriculum is assessed in quite a different way to the previous curriculum. Separate attainment targets banded in levels for each subject have been removed. In the current curriculum attainment targets are referred to in this simple way:

> By the end of each key stage, pupils are expected to know, apply and understand the matters, skills and processes specified in the relevant programme of study.

(DfE, 2014)

However, even with this change, some of the challenges of assessing computing and technology use in school will remain. As CAS/Naace (2013, p22) indicate,

> There are certainly some challenges to assessing computing.
>
> - It's hard for teachers to judge pupils' knowledge and understanding based on the outcomes of practical tasks alone.

- *If pupils work collaboratively, it can be hard to identify each individual's contribution.*

- *If the teaching of computing is embedded in other subjects, it's often difficult to separate attainment in computing from that in the host subject.*

As with any other subject, a range of assessment for learning strategies can be used to allow children to self- and peer assess their progress. In KS1 this presents more of a challenge – however, with careful guidance children will be able to start using 'value' statements about how they feel about their own achievement. Formative assessment of this nature can then be clearly matched to identification of the objectives of each intended session.

The current curriculum may provide some challenges to summative assessment due to the lack of detail in the Programme of Study. A major focus of the computing curriculum is computer science. However, the Programme of Study for both KS1 and KS2 includes only general statements, even for this area. CAS (2012) has produced its own version of a computing curriculum, which breaks down computer science into more detailed objectives. This, combined with the assessment table in the CAS/Naace (2013) document (p25), should provide a good starting point for teachers to plan a progression of experiences for children.

As with any curriculum subject it may be necessary to plan learning events specifically to ensure curriculum coverage. One of the criticisms of teachers' approach to the previous ICT curriculum subject was lack of rigour and coverage of all strands of the subject. This could indeed be the same with the current computing curriculum. There must be a focus on ensuring rigour and coverage of all areas of the curriculum. This would ideally be embedded within thematic work as well as a specific focus on ways of assessing digital literacy. It may also be necessary to design learning activities and sequences of events to allow the opportunity to assess achievement.

Including all learners

One of the final chapters in this book (Chapter 10) has a specific focus on how technology can be used to increase accessibility and extend opportunities for all learners to be successful in school. However, if we focus on the lesson idea that has been discussed in this chapter, it may be useful to think of how this approach can allow all learners to present their ideas and be successful.

The lesson idea in this chapter allows children to express their ideas by combining a range of modes of communication. Children were able to record their initial ideas about the story as well as plan and write their stories using conventional written approaches such as workbooks, whiteboards, sticky notes and the like. However, at the same time other tools were introduced to allow children to express ideas using non-textual means. Simple audio tools such as Talk Time cards and talking tins were used to let children record their initial ideas. An online 'sticky note' website Wallwisher (now known as Padlet) was used to record ideas that could be collected together to share easily – this included some images, audio files and weblinks.

The overall outcome for this project was to produce an audio soundscape, portraying an image/painting. Whilst children created their stories using text, their final 'scripts' for recording changed as they manipulated their ideas to suit the image they wanted to portray. Fisher *et al.* (2012) include a framework, which they suggest forms the major categories of ways in which technology supports learning. One of the key categories in this framework is that of knowledge building, a constructivist-influenced discussion, which includes the important area of *representing understanding in multimodal and dynamic ways* (p314).

An important implication of this paper is the impact of technology in allowing children to represent ideas and understanding in a range of ways. Allowing children to express ideas using textual, audio and visual modes then allows meaning to be made in quite different ways from perhaps just textual ways. Multimodalities, as defined by Kress (2010), suggest that the mode of communication can allow certain intrinsic characteristics to be formed when using that way of expressing meaning. Essentially, restricting children to show what they know just using text or unprepared oral tools may not allow the richness and creativity of their understanding to be shown.

Reflective questions

- How am I using digital tools across the curriculum?

- Do I allow children to use information from a range of digital sources?

- Do I have a 'bank' of resources I can use to inform my planning?

Summary

The lesson idea within this chapter is focused on the approach of allowing children to express their ideas and understanding using a range of different modes of communication. The idea discussed was carefully designed to combine an audio response to a static image, thus allowing reflection not distracted by moving images or mediated by text. A key area of the discussion focused on the need for teachers to develop their own awareness of the range of tools that are available to allow digital information to be accessed, processed and formed into digital artefacts. The underlying philosophy of this approach is widening access to communication for all learners.

We have provided some resources in this chapter that could be investigated further. Other resources, including a range of tablet apps, are included in other chapters. This is an area of the computing curriculum that could be most neglected if the focus of use of technology is merely to achieve the 'main' computer science objectives in the Programme of Study. This is also an area that needs to be achieved in an embedded way across the curriculum.

Useful links

http://sounds.bl.uk/environment/soundscapes

https://soundcloud.com/groups/soundscapes

www.freesound.org

www.nationalgallery.org.uk/initial-teacher-education/primary/learning/vernet.aspx

www.nationalgallery.org.uk/initial-teacher-education/primary/learning/zoom_vernet.html

www.soundboard.com

www.takeonepicture.org

Further reading

Barber, D and Cooper, L (2012) *Using New Web Tools in the Primary Classroom: A Practical Guide for Enhancing Teaching and Learning*. London: Routledge.

Turvey, K, Potter, J, Allen, J and Sharp, J (2014) *Primary Computing and ICT: Knowledge, Understanding and Practice*. London: SAGE/Learning Matters.

References

Buckler, S and Castle, P (2013) *Psychology for Teachers*. London: SAGE.

CAS (2012) *Computer Science: A Curriculum for Schools*. Available online at: www.computingatschool.org.uk/data/uploads/ComputingCurric.pdf (accessed 21 February 2014).

CAS/Naace (2013) *Computing in the National Curriculum: A Guide for Primary Teachers*. Available online at: http://goo.gl/GH95V7 (accessed 20 December 2016).

DfE (2014) *National Curriculum in England: Computing Programmes of Study*. Available online at: www.gov.uk/government/publications/national-curriculum-in-england-computing-programmes-of-study/national-curriculum-in-england-computing-programmes-of-study#key-stage-2 (accessed 21 February 2014).

Fisher, T, Denning, T, Higgins, C and Loveless, A (2012) Teachers knowing how to use technology: exploring a conceptual framework for purposeful learning activity. *Curriculum Journal*, 23 (3), 307–25. Available online at: www.tandfonline.com/doi/full/10.1080/09585176.2012.703492#.UvfBqf3NW80 (accessed 20 December 2016).

Horst, SW (1996) *Symbols, Computation and Intentionality: A Critique of the Computational Theory of Mind.* Berkeley, CA: University of California Press.

Kress, GR (2010) *Multimodality: A Social Semiotic Approach to Contemporary Communication.* London: Routledge.

McGregor, D (2007) *Developing Thinking, Developing Learning.* London: McGraw Hill.

TES (2014) 'Irritated' Wilshaw writes to inspectors to tell them not to prescribe 'teaching styles'. Available online at: **http://news.tes.co.uk/b/ofsted-watch/2014/01/27/sir-michael-wilshaw-forced-to-write-missive-to-inspectors-spelling-out-existing-policy.aspx** (accessed 21 February 2014).

Chapter 4

Programming in KS2

use computational thinking and creativity to understand and change the world

Learning outcomes

By the end of this chapter you should be able to:

- introduce computer programming skills using the visual programming tool Scratch;
- link computing activities to real-world examples and to other curriculum subjects;
- understand a number of basic programming constructs.

Teachers' Standards

Working through this chapter will help you meet the following standards:

1b. Set goals that stretch and challenge pupils of all backgrounds, abilities and dispositions.
2c. Guide pupils to reflect on the progress they have made and their emerging needs.
4b. Promote a love of learning and children's intellectual curiosity.
4e. Contribute to the design and provision of an engaging curriculum.

Links to the National Curriculum

Pupils should learn to:

- design, write and debug programs that accomplish specific goals;
- solve problems by decomposing them into smaller parts;
- use sequence, selection and repetition in programs; work with variables;
- use logical reasoning to explain how some simple algorithms work and to detect and correct errors in algorithms and programs.

Introduction

Children are used to interacting with games and animations on their computers and other digital devices. Many children are also used to manipulating media to make digital artefacts such as narrated slideshows and ebooks. But they are much less familiar with adding dynamic interactivity to these artefacts. Programming opens up many more possibilities by turning their simple graphics, animations, stories, music and sounds into dynamic and responsive creations that 'do something' when clicked: interactive greetings cards and collages, branching stories with choices, games with scores, animations that can be controlled using the arrow keys or mouse, or that have characters who ask questions and talk back. Sounds complicated? It doesn't need to be.

From Key Stage 1 (KS1) onwards, children are expected to create computer programs so that they get a better understanding of how the devices and websites they encounter work and of the role of technology in our lives today. To do this, they need to understand basic concepts, such as that an algorithm is a sequence of instructions; that when an algorithm is coded as a program a digital device can be controlled, and so on.

The free programming tool Scratch, developed by the Media Lab at the Massachusetts Institute of Technology (MIT), is a great place to explore these ideas. It is colourful, engaging and relatively easy to use, and is one of several visual programming languages that make use of coloured blocks to create algorithms. The very name Scratch is derived from the disc jockey technique of scratching, which involves manipulating vinyl recordings to create samples of sounds that can be mixed together in different combinations. We can do just that with samples of code on the computer by adding scripts to objects or 'sprites' to make them behave in various ways. This can be as simple as making a character move and speak to tell a story, or you can use it in more complex ways to manipulate scientific and mathematical variables.

The power and simplicity of Scratch programming enables you to teach computing concepts and techniques whilst staying true to the ethos of purposeful activity that is the hallmark of good teaching. This allows computing to become an expressive tool that can be used right across the primary curriculum for solving problems and making interactive media that are connected in meaningful ways to children's interests and curriculum topics. The emphasis is on children as digital makers and inventors. As Mitch Resnick from MIT explains,

> We find that active members of the Scratch community start to think of themselves differently. They begin to see themselves as creators and designers, as people who can make things with digital media, not just browse, chat, and play games. While many people can read digital media, Scratchers can write digital media.

(Resnick, 2013)

This new focus on understanding how things work and on applying that knowledge to 'make' and 'do' means that computing is an exciting and inventive environment. And the fact that Scratch is based on a graphical representation of code makes it much more accessible than programming languages that use written code. Another plus is that Scratch projects are remixable and shareable, meaning that children can reuse ideas from other members of the Scratch community to make projects for a ready-made audience.

Lesson idea: remix with Scratch

In order to use computing creatively children need to have direct experience of manipulating code. A visual programming language such as Scratch makes it easier to put together sequences of instructions by snapping together coloured blocks to assemble a script. This lesson idea explores how you can adapt existing scripts to create your own customised projects on a range of curriculum themes.

Things you need

- Scratch Online (**https://scratch.mit.edu**) or the Scratch 2.0 offline editor (free to download);

- a set of laminated Scratch blocks (find some examples here: **http://scratched.gse. harvard.edu/resources/vector-scratch-blocks**);

- sticky notes or an online whiteboard such as Padlet (**http://padlet.com**).

Before you start

If this is the first time you have visited the Scratch website (**http://scratch.mit.edu**), take some time to look around. Clicking 'Create' will take you into the programming environment. Here you will notice that the screen has four parts: a blocks palette where all the colour-coded blocks are stored; a sprite list showing the objects you are manipulating; a stage where you can see your ideas taking shape; and a scripts area where you build projects by snapping together blocks to tell your sprites what to do. This 'drag and snap' capability encourages young learners to experiment without the need to write complex code, allowing them to be creative and successful straight away.

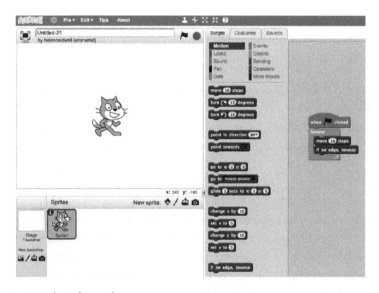

Figure 4.1   A screenshot of Scratch

All new projects begin with a cat sprite on the stage. You have the option to delete the cat and add sprites and backdrops from the libraries or upload or draw your own. Another important idea is that one sprite can have several poses or 'costumes', making it easy to animate.

A good starting place is the Scratch Help page (**http://scratch.mit.edu/help**), which has a step-by-step introduction and some starter projects that give you an idea of the range of projects you can make. For example, you could add a photo of yourself to an animated dance party or use video sensing to activate sounds using hand gestures and a webcam.

Notice that each starter project comes with instructions and remix ideas. If you click on 'See inside', you can explore the blocks of code and look at how they are put together. Scroll down the project page and you find many remix examples; these can provide useful models showing how others have solved the challenges.

It is also worth downloading the Getting Started Guide and laminating the set of Scratch cards on the Help page. The cards cover a number of basic techniques, such as adding sound and animation effects. Distribute these and ask your class to show you what they can do with a sprite and you will be surprised by the variety of projects they create.

Make sure to join Scratch and create a class login so that you can save and share your projects. And as you explore these tools with children, remember that you don't have to be an expert coder yourself; you can learn more advanced techniques alongside your pupils and develop your own skills by adapting and remixing other people's projects just as they do.

You will find it useful to become familiar with the Scratch components shown in Table 4.1.

Table 4.1 What Scratch components can do

Scratch component	What it is	Useful to know
Sprite	An individual character or object	You can draw your own, select from a library or import from the web
Script	A short program which instructs sprites to do things	Scripts can be attached to backdrops as well as sprites
Command block	Blocks stack together to make a program	You can move, nest, separate, delete and duplicate blocks. Click to test out a block or stack
Stage	The area where you place sprites and test programs.	The stage is a grid and you can specify sprites' coordinates on the stage
Backdrop	The stage has backdrops that can also be programmed	You can draw your own, import or select from a library
Costume	Sprites can have several poses, called costumes	Changing costumes lets you animate sprites

Context

These lesson ideas can be used as a standalone lesson with follow-up activities, or a couple of shorter lessons, aimed at Year 4, 5 or 6 classes. This lesson assumes that children have been introduced to Scratch, and that they have had some experience using Scratch cards and can make a sprite change colour, move to a beat, say something and follow the mouse.

Learning outcomes for this lesson

Pupils will:

- understand that programs respond to precise sequences of instructions;

- gain experience of the computational practice of reusing and remixing code;

- find out that it is important to add and test small amounts of code at once;

- learn to apply the make–test–debug sequence;

- experience coding as a creative activity.

Lesson outline

Remix with Scratch

In this lesson children explore the Scratch Starter Projects: **http://scratch.mit.edu/ starter_projects**. They talk about how code is constructed through a hands-on activity away from the computer and then choose a Scratch project to remix by adding their own ideas (Table 4.2).

Table 4.2 Group work with Scratch

Lesson sequence	Organisation	Resources
Starter	Children in mixed-ability groups of four	Prepared envelopes of laminated Scratch blocks
Main lesson	Children working together in mixed-ability pairs	Laptops, netbooks or computers Webcams Microphones
Plenary	Children together as a whole group	Sticky notes Online working wall (e.g. Padlet) or a place to post notes

Starter: following a script

Assign children to one of six groups relating to the themes on the Scratch Starter Projects webpage: 'Animation', 'Games', 'Interactive Art', 'Music and Dance', 'Stories' and 'Video Sensing'. Each theme offers a choice of four activities.

Give the groups envelopes containing laminated Scratch blocks, such as 'move', 'point towards', 'turn', 'say', 'switch costume', 'play sound', 'change tempo', 'when clicked', 'repeat' and 'forever'.

Ask the children to assemble their blocks to make a script. Within their groups, children choose roles as 'sprites' or 'coders' and role-play their sequence of instructions as a short drama. They find out which instructions the sprites are able to follow and see the need to make precise sequences. This will help to develop the vocabulary they need to describe how they solved a coding problem and allow them to make predictions before they try out their ideas on the computer.

Main lesson: Scratch remix

In pairs, pupils explore a selection of the projects on the Starter Projects page (**http://scratch.mit.edu/starter_projects**). Each pair is given a category of four projects to explore within 'Animation', 'Games', 'Interactive Art', 'Music and Dance', 'Stories' and 'Video Sensing' (Figure 4.2).

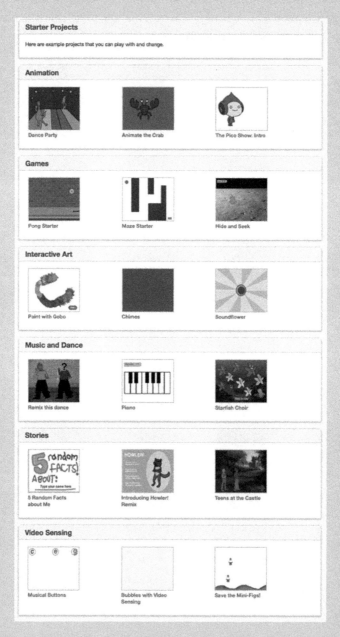

Figure 4.2   Screenshots of Scratch starter projects

These example projects cover a range of applications from simple animations and stories to quirky ways of making music, art tools that respond to sound and Kinect-style games activated by gestures. Pupils choose one project to look at more closely. They investigate the scripts and prepare a spoken explanation of what is happening as they play the project. Selected pairs then describe and demonstrate their scripts to the class.

In the next part of the lesson, the teacher points out the remix ideas for each project and models how to change sprites and backdrops and how to add sounds. The ideas of incremental problem solving (developing each bit and trying it out) and debugging (finding and fixing mistakes) are introduced, and children are encouraged to follow a 'make–test–debug' sequence.

Following on from this, pupils go back to their selected project and make changes using the example remixes to help them.

Critical questions to ask pupils:

- Do your blocks need to be assembled in a certain order?
- What other blocks could you use?
- Which instructions does your sprite respond to?
- Can you simplify your script? How does this help?
- Are there alternative ways of writing your script?
- How did you identify and fix problems?
- Does analysing other people's code help you to write your own?
- What are the key blocks for your theme?
- How do the key blocks differ across the project themes?

Commentary

Prompt cards could be at hand to help children who need a visual reminder of how to add sounds, sprites and backdrops. Extension activities might include adding a surprise action to the project or comparing two themes to find out which are the most important blocks in each genre of projects.

Plenary

Selected pairs demonstrate their remixed projects and talk through the changes they have made. Each project is opened in full screen and children move around the room trying out each other's projects. They are encouraged to look at the code, ask questions and give constructive feedback. At the end of the lesson children leave sticky notes on a working wall, consisting of 'I can' and 'Can I?' sentences highlighting achievements and identifying one aspect of their project to take forwards in the next lesson. An alternative is to capture reflection at the end of the lesson by posting to an online wall such as Padlet (**http://padlet.com**). This technique could also provide extra support during the lesson as children post and answer each other's queries.

Next steps

The remixed projects might be uploaded to a class blog or website, or shared via the Scratch community so that others can play them, allowing for wider feedback.

Assessment

Assessing learning during the lesson helps to ensure that suitable challenges are in place for all. Look for opportunities for mini-plenaries, peer review and feedback during the development of the Scratch projects. Help to make learning visible by creating opportunities for talk partners and modelling the appropriate use of computing vocabulary so that children gain expertise in evaluating their own progress. Screencasting apps such as ShowMe and Explain Everything enable children to record and share their strategies for solving coding problems, and the results provide useful evidence of achievement. Alternatively, children might keep project journals reflecting on the development of their ideas and emergent problem-solving approaches. The exit sticky notes from this lesson will be available for review at the beginning of the next: they could be used to involve children in compiling differentiated success criteria to match the learning objective. Activities such as these all help to develop a shared understanding of what makes a good Scratch project and build metacognition, so that children are more explicitly aware of their learning.

Taking it further

In this lesson we explored a range of Scratch project themes in order to get a feel for computing as a creative activity. Future lessons are likely to concentrate on just one theme, such as animation, stories or perhaps an aspect of science or mathematics. Think about identifying a theme that sits well with a topic you are already studying. For example, you could choose to make games around curriculum topics such as healthy eating, road safety, geographical landmarks or books. Your pupils could spend time storyboarding project ideas and integrating their knowledge of a subject. Peer review of the storyboards would help to identify potential challenges and help make the projects manageable. You could provide support by putting together a portfolio of example projects sourced from the Scratch website that match your theme and identify useful blocks. For example, certain blocks such as the 'broadcast/when I receive' and 'say/wait' pairs of blocks are crucial for getting characters to talk to each other in an animation or story, whereas being able to create a variable is essential for keeping scores or timers in a game. The Creative Computing Guide from the ScratchEd Team at MIT lists useful sets of blocks for games, stories and arts-themed projects (ScratchEd Team, 2011). The Barefoot Computing site has a good collection of cross-curricular ideas (**http://barefootcas.org.uk**).

Scratch offers opportunities across all subjects and has a strong affinity with many maths concepts, such as creating number machines, investigating shapes and angles, calculating change or using coordinates. Find examples on Phil Bagge's excellent site, Junior Computer Science (**http://code-it.co.uk**), and think about how motivated children will be to learn about coordinates, variables and random numbers if they need them to control the speed, direction and angle of a catapulted 'angry bird' in the context of a game that they have designed themselves. Once children are engaged with a project, you can then seek to identify opportunities to reinforce computational thinking skills, as Steve Hunt suggests in a Computing At School article:

> *A grasp of CT {computational thinking} enables people to see the world through a computational lens. Computational thinkers gain an understanding of the world about them that makes them able to model things from a variety of perspectives, each of which brings out some computational aspect of what they see.*

(Hunt, 2014)

Activity

Do you know your way around Scratch? Look at the screenshot in Figure 4.3 and see if you can identify the following items:

Stage area	Blocks palette	Scripts are	Sprite list	A backdrop
Project title	Grow and shrink tools	A sprite		

(Continued)

(Continued)

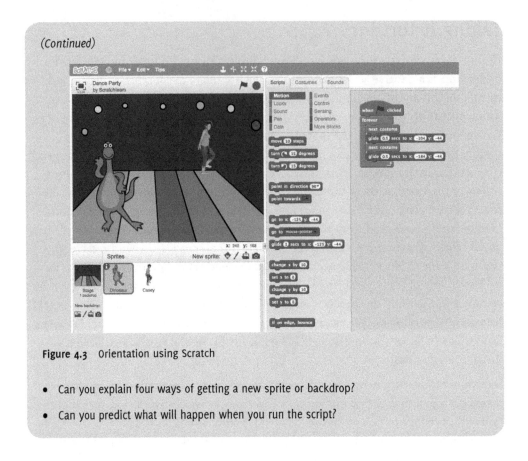

Figure 4.3 Orientation using Scratch

- Can you explain four ways of getting a new sprite or backdrop?

- Can you predict what will happen when you run the script?

Discussion

Scratch across the curriculum

Once your class has got to grips with the basics, you can begin to use Scratch for making exciting digital artefacts that demonstrate children's learning about various curriculum topics as they design and write programs that accomplish specific goals. Not only do they gain programming skills and engage in collaborative problem solving, they demonstrate their growing subject knowledge by turning it into interactive content. Rather than being a discrete set of 'lessons on computing', creative computing can thus be aligned in a purposeful way with other learning objectives.

For example, each of the Scratch project themes considered in this lesson has cross-curricular potential, as follows.

Animation

- Present a pivotal scene from history.

- Demonstrate how to handle a playground confrontation.

- Animate a set of creatures in their habitat.

- Prepare a quiz on a historical period.

Games

- Create a science game sorting animals and their habitats.

- Devise a maths game where a shark eats all the even-numbered fish.

- Create a number machine puzzle.

- Make a 'beat the clock' game converting Fahrenheit to Celsius or pounds to euros.

Interactive art

- Use art tools to create a Mondrian-style composition.

- Explore the geometric patterns of Islamic art using turtle graphics.

- Recreate a scene from a book.

- Design an interactive birthday card.

Music and dance

- Use sound and movement to demonstrate a molecular reaction.

- Design a voice-activated soundscape based on a book setting.

- Build an interactive band by combining sprites and sounds.

Stories

- Make a 'choose the ending' story based on a traditional tale.

- Use text and narration to tell a five-photo news story.

- Animate language features such as alliteration or onomatopoeia.

Video sensing

- Sort food into 'healthy' and 'unhealthy' using hand gestures.

- Make a gesture-based spelling game based on alphabet bubbles.

- Use your hand to pause a scrolling set of objects and name an object in French.

Once children have gained some experience within a project genre they can apply their skills to pursue an idea based on their own interests in a more self-directed way.

However, having students pursuing different paths poses a challenge and you will need to give thought to structuring lessons around key questions such as:

- What part of your project will you be working on today?

- Where would you like to get to today?

- What might you need help with?

- Who might be able to help you?

- What aspects would you like feedback about?

Providing support

The fact that creative computing is open-ended and best developed in a workshop style of environment can be a challenge. Children learn to program at different speeds and you may have to give up the role of being the expert as some pupils get hooked and take projects in directions beyond what you had envisaged. Others will find coding more challenging, but given a supportive environment all will make and learn something new each lesson. The ease with which you can take apart and remix blocks allows you to create scaffolded learning opportunities for a range of abilities in Scratch. Try to think of ways of simplifying the task for those who need it, perhaps by working with a limited selection of blocks, by solving a smaller problem within a project, by continuing to develop a template or by dismantling projects to see how they are made. As our example lesson demonstrates, a starting point is to change the characters, setting or theme within an existing project, or to introduce one skill at a time, such as a time limit or a score within a gaming theme.

Ways of supporting beginning programmers

- Provide a finished project to play and dissect, together with a folder of characters, sprites and sound effects for children to construct their own version.
- Load a completed game and experiment with simple enhancements.
- Offer challenges: 'What can you make with ten blocks?' or 'Add a surprise'.
- Find the errors and debug a sample project.
- Provide a template and ask children to continue the story, add questions to the quiz or add enemies to the game.
- Use a pair programming approach, with teams of two taking turns at being driver and navigator, one using the keyboard and one identifying problems and making suggestions.
- Use an online wall such as Padlet for pupils to post and answer queries during the lesson.

You will need to encourage your pupils to trial, debug and refine their projects. This ongoing process of developing and testing is known as being iterative and incremental. Children will enjoy the challenge of being given a partly completed project to finish, test and debug. Fixing problems through systematic debugging in this way, rather than by trial and error, is satisfying and children will be interested to learn that the term is associated with a real bug causing a problem by flying into a computer in 1945.

Above all, you need to encourage problem solving and solution sharing, and know when it is timely to offer assistance. Children respond well to an approach through which they think of an idea, look at what others have done, create a prototype, get feedback and redesign. Rather than giving them the answers, you can help by providing project planning and feedback sheets, posting discussion topics and setting time aside for peer feedback and testing. Working towards the finished artefact is the goal and it is important to recognise children's achievements by publishing and sharing. You could consider holding a celebration event at the end of a unit of work: guests, music, snacks, badges and awards can all help create an atmosphere of success.

Computational thinking and creative computing

While your class is busy inventing Scratch art, stories, games, music, maths activities and animations, you need to look for opportunities to draw out key computational ideas so that they can learn to apply these techniques more widely. This is an idea explored by Jeanette Wing from Carnegie Mellon University:

> *Computational thinking is a way of solving problems, designing systems, and understanding human behavior that draws on concepts fundamental to computer science.*

(Wing, 2012)

Research suggests that young programmers struggle with the broader concepts if they just learn coding without generalising their thinking (Meerbaum-Salant *et al.*, 2011). In order to develop transferable thinking skills alongside knowledge of coding, they need to understand more than how to create their programs; they need to find out why a particular solution is the best. Computational thinkers need to be able to use terms such as algorithms, conditionals, loops and events to describe their coding activities. It is difficult to take these concepts on board if they are taught in isolation: children need to understand why they are useful, see examples in context and, most importantly, see how they are relevant to the programs they have written themselves. It is therefore better to highlight programming concepts in a meaningful context such as making a game where you need to use them to keep score, launch a projectile, detect collisions and create enemies. Other useful ways of reinforcing terms and concepts are through 'unplugged' activities away from the computer and through finding real-world examples.

The computational terms given in Table 4.3 are particularly relevant when working in Scratch.

Table 4.3   Useful computational terms with Scratch

Term	What it means	Examples
Algorithm	Combining instructions into a *sequence* to achieve a goal Algorithms may be *decomposed* into smaller parts or *procedures* to make them easier to understand	Write a recipe Instruct a remote-control toy to navigate a maze Animate a sprite to draw a square
Loop	Repeating a sequence. Types of loops include 'until', 'while' or 'forever' loops that run until something changes as a condition is met	An electrical circuit A dancing sprite
Conditional selection	Conditional statements execute code depending on what happens to other objects based on conditions such as 'if this ... then that' or 'if ... else'	A room thermostat responding to temperature changes *If* the answer is correct, say 'well done'; *else* say 'try again' Collision detection in a game: *If* 'touching black' *then* 'hide'
Pattern recognition	Repeats in designs or similar qualities that are shared by a number of different items. We can implement a pattern again in a different context	Making a football move across a field is just like making a bird fly Detecting whether an arrow hits a target is the same as detecting if a player caught a ball
Abstraction	Removing unnecessary detail so you can concentrate on the bigger picture by putting together collections of smaller parts	The London Underground map A school timetable Using pen blocks with repeated functions to create complex patterns using simple polygons
Variables	Things that can change while a program is running	Games make variables more concrete as they control the state of a sprite, e.g. 'score', 'number of questions', 'speed', 'lives'
Initialisation	Setting variables to their starting values	Set the score to zero at the beginning of a game Establish a starting position for a sprite
Event handling	One event causing another to happen	Responding to someone talking during a conversation In Scratch, broadcast 'The game has begun' and display sprites Use the 'broadcast' and 'when I receive' block pair to coordinate sprites' actions
Parallelism	Making events happen at the same time, as opposed to sequential programming in which events execute consecutively	Act out a series of instructions highlighting things happening at the same time, e.g. walking and talking A single sprite can do multiple things at once and multiple sprites can also perform actions simultaneously

For further explanations, see the explanations of computational thinking concepts and approaches on the Barefoot Computing site: http://barefootcas.org.uk/barefoot-primary-computing-resources/concepts.

Activity

See if you can think of 'unplugged' activities for three of the computational terms in the table above that demonstrate a computational concept away from technology. Examples are showing the concept of initialisation using netball players returning to their start positions after scoring or writing an algorithm to play Snakes and Ladders.

Reflective questions

- Think about how the introduction of Scratch programming sits alongside other computing activities. Can you describe a progression of skills across Key Stages?

- Can you identify a selection of hardware and software needed to practise computational thinking in a range of contexts?

- What are the implications of teachers adopting a role as a 'guide on the side' rather than as a 'sage on the stage'?

Summary

We have thought about the use of Scratch as an expressive learning environment rather than just a place to learn to write code. The chance to make music videos, animated stories, adventure games and quizzes adds a new dimension by turning 'learning by doing' into 'learning by making'. As children explore programming as a tool to make meaningful artefacts, they can also be helped to develop logical thinking skills and understand the technologies that surround them. A prescriptive scheme of ready-made lessons will not achieve this depth of understanding. Instead, we need to promote computing as a way of thinking and allow time to play with the tools in an inventive way. Just as the act of writing with pen and paper helps us think, the process of using programming tools can lead children to refine and reflect on their ideas. As one Scratch project leads to another, children learn skills that are useful for everyone, everywhere: how to analyse problems, apply maths concepts, edit and debug, communicate with others and design logical solutions. In this context, our role as teachers is to help them to develop the language and concepts to articulate their thinking strategies and become better learners. As Mitch Resnick from the MIT Media Lab suggests,

> *Ultimately, what is needed is a shift in mindsets, so that people begin to see coding not only as a pathway to good jobs, but as a new form of expression and a new context for learning.*

(Resnick, 2013)

Useful links

Code.org: **https://code.org/educate/curriculum/elementary-school**

Several sets of self-paced tutorials aimed at introducing computer science basics to young learners.

Scratch Ed: **http://scratched.gse.harvard.edu**

An online community of educators sharing computing resources and success stories.

Computational Thinking Illustrated: **www.ctillustrated.com**

Downloadable cartoons and explanations of computational thinking from the Galileo Academy of Science and Technology. Useful for talking about concepts such as algorithms, pattern recognition and generalisation, decomposition and modelling.

Computer Science Unplugged: **http://csunplugged.org**

A collection of free learning activities that teach computer science away from the computer through games, puzzles and physical activities.

Digital Schoolhouse: **www.digitalschoolhouse.org.uk**

A nationally recognised project for the teaching of computer science with lesson resources to download for KS1 and KS2.

Junior Computer Science: **www.code-it.co.uk**

An extensive collection of resources provided by Computing At School master teacher, Phil Bagge, including sample schemes of work and Phil's views on why computing is important for primary pupils.

Thinking Myself: **http://games.thinkingmyself.com**

Activities and games explaining decomposition, patterns, abstraction and algorithms.

Further reading

Creative Computing: an introductory computing curriculum using Scratch. Available online at: **http://scratched.gse.harvard.edu/guide** (accessed 20 December 2016).

154 editable pages of plans, activities and strategies for teaching creative computing, including a workbook version aimed at learners.

Getting started with Scratch. Available online at: **www.raspberrypi.org/learning/getting-started-with-scratch** (accessed 20 December 2016).

Learning resources from the Raspberry Pi Foundation.

Papert, S (1980) *Mindstorms: Children, Computers, and Powerful Ideas*. New York: Basic Books.

Resnick, M (2012) *Reviving Papert's Dream*. Available online at: **http://web.media.mit.edu/~mres/papers/educational-technology-2012.pdf** (accessed 24 October 2016).

References

Bagge, P (2013) *Death by Scratch*. Available online at: **http://code-it-cs.blogspot.co.uk/2013/11/death-by-scratch.html** (accessed 24 October 2016).

Hunt, S (2014) *Computational Thinking: A Special Way to Look at Problems*. Available online at: **www.computingatschool.org.uk/data/uploads/newsletter-spring-2014.pdf** (accessed 24 October 2016).

Meerbaum-Salant, O, Armoni, M and Ben-Ari, M (2011) Habits of programming in Scratch. In: *Proceedings of the 16th Annual Joint Conference on Innovation and Technology in Computer Science Education*, pp168–72. Darmstadt, Germany: ACM.

Resnick, M (2013) *Learn to Code, Code to Learn: How Programming Prepares Kids for More Than Math*. Available online at: **www.edsurge.com/n/2013-05-08-learn-to-code-code-to-learn** (accessed 24 October 2016).

ScratchEd Team (2011) *Scratch Curriculum Guide*. Available online at: **http://scratched.media.mit.edu/resources/scratch-curriculum-guide-draft** (accessed 24 October 2016).

Wing, J (2012) *What Is Computational Thinking?* Available online at: **www.cs.cmu.edu/~CompThink** (accessed 24 October 2016).

Chapter 5

Physical computing in KS2

computing has deep links with mathematics, science and design and technology, and provides insights into both natural and artificial systems

---

Learning outcomes

By the end of this chapter you should be able to:

- explain what is meant by physical computing and its relevance to the computing curriculum;
- suggest ways to help children design and write programs that accomplish specific goals, including controlling or simulating physical systems;
- explore and compare control hardware and software devices to develop programs using sensors, motors and robots.

Teachers' Standards

Working through this chapter will help you meet the following standards:

1a. Establish a safe and stimulating environment.
1b. Set goals that stretch and challenge pupils.
4e. Contribute to the design and provision of an engaging curriculum.

Links to the National Curriculum

Pupils should learn to:

- design, write and debug programs that accomplish specific goals, including controlling or simulating physical systems;
- recognise common uses of information technology beyond school.

Introduction

Children love making things. How about a piano made of carrots? A jelly baby that screams? A human beatbox choir? Or a game controller made of Play-Doh? Combine some electronics tinkering with a basic knowledge of Scratch programming and you are into the magical world of physical computing where you can build all manner of contraptions and write code to control them. This chapter looks at how children can apply their computing knowledge to the physical world to 'make something that does something'. In it, we will explore computing projects that use control devices and invention kits.

By exploring the impact that program instructions have on the physical world, we can highlight the ways that digital devices influence how we live: microwaves, TV controllers, alarm clocks, phones, SatNav systems, supermarket scanners, burglar alarms and Kinect games, to name but a few. When you think about it, children are rarely far away from a digital device of one kind or another. Pursuing their own ideas and solving problems to make workable gadgets helps them understand the relevance and importance of computing to their lives, and provides clear links between computing and other subjects, such as design and technology, maths and science. Through active engagement in this type of activity, they develop thinking and problem-solving skills, and apply their computing knowledge in ways that have a visible effect in the physical world. As Tom Kenyon explains in *The Guardian*,

> *Creativity is key ... I'm delighted that computer science is going to be taught in classrooms, and that its rigour as a discipline has been recognised. But beyond rigour I'm interested in the power of computing to link science and art, creativity and engineering ... The way to do this is to learn from Britain's digital heroes and to make fun, exciting and useful things.*

(Kenyon, 2013)

Lesson idea: wacky inventions

In this unit of three lessons, students work with the Raspberry Pi, Makey Makey kits and the Scratch programming language to create unusual musical instruments and game controllers using everyday objects such as vegetables and Play-Doh.

Things you need

- Makey Makey (approximately £40);

- Raspberry Pi (approximately £30);

- Scratch (free);

- a selection of conductive materials (e.g. Play-Doh, tinfoil, water, fruit, vegetables, graphite pencils, sweets, people, coins, cutlery);

- craft resources such as paper and card.

Before you start

This lesson assumes that you have a basic knowledge of the free Scratch programming software. If you need to brush up on this there is an excellent step-by-step introduction and some starter projects to explore in the Help section of the Scratch website (**http://scratch.mit.edu/help**).

You also need to be familiar with the Makey Makey Classic invention kit (**makeymakey.com**) and the Raspberry Pi computer (**www.raspberrypi.org**). A Makey Makey consists of a two-sided circuit board, which plugs into a computer. One side has a simple set of inputs for up, down, left and right arrow keys, space bar and left mouse click. The other side gives you access to 12 more keys. You use crocodile clips to connect the board to objects that can conduct an electric current and you hold the earth clip in your fingers to complete the circuit to the earth bar on the board. The objects can be anything that can carry a small current: fruit, water, foil and fingers all work well.

The Raspberry Pi is a small, cheap computer. It works well with the Makey Makey and is great for getting children interested in how computers work. Both the Makey Makey and the Raspberry Pi can be used in combination with programming languages such as Scratch or Python. However, if you don't have a Raspberry Pi you can use the Makey Makey with any computer. You can find a quickstart guide here: **www.sparkfun.com/tutorials/378**.

Context

This series of three lessons introduces the idea of physical computing using the Makey Makey, Raspberry Pi and Scratch. The lessons might be used as a unit of work or as part of a carousel of activities on a curriculum enrichment day.

Learning outcomes for this series of lessons

Pupils will:

- understand that programs respond to different sorts of inputs;
- learn that one object can be used to control another;
- experiment with the effects of changing conditions and variables;
- build understanding of how parts of a computer work together.

Unit outline

Lesson 1

This lesson begins with an unplugged activity (i.e. with no digital equipment) to highlight that a computer system is composed of parts, each with its own function. Groups of children are given a physical object to analyse. The objects you choose need to be simple examples that have several parts relating to a whole; for example, a shoe (which has a heel, a toe and laces), a bell, a whisk or a stapler. Children begin by examining their object, looking at all its parts individually, describing what each part does and explaining how each contributes to the whole. They go on to think about how they might repurpose their object by redesigning it to be something else. What extra parts could they add? What changes could they make to the parts to make the object do something new?

Next, the children are given a Raspberry Pi and a set of labels. This leads to a discussion about how parts of a computer work together and to a simple explanation of terms relating to inputs and outputs.

Each group links their Raspberry Pi to a monitor, mouse and keyboard, opens Scratch and experiments with the blocks they are given on a laminated Scratch card. A set of simple Scratch cards can be found in the Help section of the Scratch website (**http:// scratch.mit.edu/help/cards**). Pupils are encouraged to find an aspect of their Scratch activity to change or remix, just as they did with their physical objects at the beginning of the lesson. This emphasises the computational practice of reusing and remixing, making something new by building on existing ideas (Brennan and Resnick, 2012).

The lesson ends with a discussion of how the Scratch blocks fit together to achieve a purpose. Groups explain how they have inputted information into their program to guide a sprite and how the output is shown on the screen and through the speakers if there is a sound. This is related to other input and output contexts such as the voice- and gesture-activated inputs on the Scratch website, touch screen devices, and ways in which sensors interact with data in systems such as a central heating thermostat or a burglar alarm.

Lesson 2

This lesson begins by connecting together the Raspberry Pi, a monitor and a Makey Makey. Guided by images from the Makey Makey Quick Start Guide (**www. MakeyMakey.com/howto.php**), children connect one end of a crocodile clip to 'Earth' on the front of the kit and another to 'Space' to complete the circuit. They can now make the cursor move in a word-processing program by touching the clip to complete the circuit and activate the space bar. The next step is to attach the clip to an object and write a simple Scratch script (Figure 5.1) instructing the computer to make a sound when the space bar is pressed.

Figure 5.1 Writing a simple Scratch script

Children can now import from the Scratch sprite and sound libraries to make unusual objects using a selection of conductive materials. For example, they could make a banana cowbell, an apple bass drum, or a cymbal crash when two friends who are connected to the Makey Makey touch hands to do a high-five. By activating two keys using crocodile clips they can explore imaginative combinations such as a banana that talks to an orange or a singing jelly baby duo.

Moving on from this, children might try connecting up to six computer keys with conductible materials to make a musical instrument such as a piano made of carrots, peppers or apples (Figure 5.2). There are example pianos on the Scratch website which can be modified to include the notes needed for simple tunes such as 'Happy Birthday',

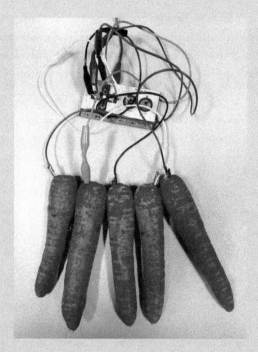

Figure 5.2 A carrot piano

Example Scratch piano project: http://scratch.mit.edu/projects/2543877

More Scratch and Makey Makey projects:

https://scratch.mit.edu/studios/223260

https://scratch.mit.edu/studios/230629

Video example: https://vine.co/v/hFVml1XwiMH

'Twinkle Twinkle' or 'Jingle Bells'. Pupils will quickly discover that they can play chords and can combine beats and raps from the Scratch sound library to make all kinds of musical compositions.

Commentary

Have a look at the tools for creating a choir of beatbox characters on the Incredibox site (www.incredibox.com/gb) and set the challenge of writing a Scratch program to control a real human beatbox choir. Children could record their own sounds or import them from the Scratch library and then get their human choir to hold the crocodile clips so that a conductor can 'play' them by tapping their hands. This idea could be modified so that each person produces a sound effect to make a storytelling machine.

Example beatbox quartet: https://scratch.mit.edu/projects/106102276

Example sound effects for storytelling: https://scratch.mit.edu/projects/11744561

The Scratch website has many other Makey Makey projects on the theme of sound and music, including drum kits and dance mats.

Once your class knows how to manipulate sounds in this way you will find that the ideas themselves take hold and the programming becomes purposeful as children pursue solutions to problems they invent themselves. Consider uploading videos of your sound and music compositions to YouTube or Vimeo so that they can be shared with an audience straight away.

Lesson 3

In this final lesson, children make a games controller by connecting the Makey Makey kit to modelling material such as Play-Doh. They use their home-made controller to play classic arcade games that involve the arrow keys and space bar, such as Tetris, Pong or Pac-Man:

www.freetetris.org/game.phpwww.childline.org.uk/Play/Games/Pages/Pong.aspx

www.thepcmanwebsite.com/media/pacman_flash

Here is a set of games that work with the Makey Makey: https://padlet.com/helencaldwell/makey.

This simple controller is made by sticking the ends of the crocodile clips into the Play-Doh and connecting them to the arrow keys via the Makey Makey. You can be more ambitious by using conductive paint or a metal tin to customise your controller, as outlined in these instructions from Coding Club: www.codingclub.co.uk/pi_controller.php.

Once you have a working controller, you can set the challenge of customising a Scratch game so that it fits a theme and works with the controller. Any sample project that uses a limited number of keys can act as a starting place. Try controlling this simple rocket: **http://scratch.mit.edu/projects/11112802**, this version of the classic Simon game: **http://scratch.mit.edu/projects/11455923** or this Super Mario game: **http://scratch.mit.edu/projects/2418711**. A search of the Scratch website using 'arrow keys' as the key words will yield many more examples.

Commentary

It is worth allowing thinking and planning time for children to choose a theme that grabs them. This will encourage them to apply their skills and solve problems as they go to produce an end product that represents their vision. You could extend the project by using the excellent Code Club resources (www.codeclub.org.uk) to develop Scratch game-making skills over a series of lessons.

The finished games can be showcased by uploading to the Scratch website, and grabbing the embed code so that they can be inserted into a class blog or website as playable games. This will lend authenticity to the work and provide fertile opportunities for giving feedback via online comments.

Taking it further

Of course you can make all kinds of things with your Makey Makey kit, especially if you combine conductive materials with craft materials. Have a look at the gallery of ideas at **http://makeymakey.com/gallery** and be sure to check out the musical guinea pigs!

Here is a selection of follow-on ideas for exploring some of the themes from this set of lessons:

- Make a 'musical buttons' instrument that plays notes in response to hand gestures via your webcam. There is a Scratch 2.0 starter project for this and many remix examples showing how you can alter the original project to fit your own ideas: **http://scratch.mit.edu/projects/10128168**.

- Combine a Lego WeDo robotics kit with the Raspberry Pi and Scratch to make your own interactive projects using the distance, light and tilt sensors and motors. Useful links include these starter resources: **http://info.scratch.mit.edu/WeDo** and ideas for storytelling from the ScratchEd team: **http://scratched.media.mit.edu/stories/we-do-wedo**.

- Use the Raspberry Pi and Scratch to program a set of radio-controlled Pi-Cars: **http://pi-cars.com**.

Discussion

Children as makers

Our emphasis in this unit of lessons has been on children as inventors combining technology skills with craft skills to make innovative products or inventions that 'do something'. Over 30 years ago Seymour Papert, founder of the Massachusetts Institute of Technology Media Lab and one of the inventors of the Logo programming language, described a 'constructionist' vision of how children might use programming skills for a range of creative activities such as controlling robots, composing music or creating games (Papert, 1980). At the time, this was a radical idea and things have moved on apace, but although some aspects of this vision are now a reality, as Resnick notes, children have still not become *truly fluent* with the use of technologies and it is *as if they can 'read' but not 'write'* (Resnick, 2012, p1). Today there is a new emphasis on the type of designing and creating that Papert envisioned, and on enabling children to express themselves creatively through programming.

Drawing on his experiences with the Constructionist Learning Lab, a technology-rich project for teens at the Maine Youth Center in 1999, Papert recognised the power of learning through making: we learn most readily and effectively when we are engaged with, and in control of, our learning, and when we are making something we really want to make. Making tangible digital devices provides a creative, purposeful and stimulating context in which children can learn about computing and can experience the power of computing to help them invent and control. It can also bring together programming in the classroom, computing at home and real-world uses of technology. Eben Upton, the inventor of the Raspberry Pi, describes his idea as an *attempt to reboot hobbyist computing for children*, something that used to be commonplace (Upton, 2012).

Playful but not easy

Taking things apart and adapting them, and making your own gadgets, is playful and fun, but it can also be demanding. Acknowledging the fact that 'fun' does not necessarily mean 'easy', Papert (1993) coined the phrase *hard fun*. As teachers, we need to show that we are learning too, and that enjoyment and hard work often go together. We can model the fact that we are prepared to encounter difficulties and to solve problems, and we can demonstrate the need to be flexible in our thinking as our ideas evolve and are tested. For the learning in your classroom to be effective, then, you will need to allow time for children to reflect and to learn from their mistakes.

Papert was an advocate of constructionism, the idea of learning through making and applying knowledge, and of involving learners in decisions about their learning. In this context, hard fun means understanding that you won't always get it right first time and that accepting feedback, rethinking and revising are all part of the learning process. It also means spending time defining the problem and developing a joint vision of what a shareable end product might look like. In the classroom situation, plenty of opportunities need to be made for children to discuss goals and to evaluate their progress towards them.

This type of approach is based upon a learning landscape where teachers and children jointly construct ideas by applying their problem-solving and computing skills in a way that leaves them with something to show for their endeavours. In order for this to be meaningful, there needs to be enough flexibility in your planning to allow children to pursue questions that they find interesting. Another crucial component is the need for a platform, event or publication that showcases the range of finished projects for reflection and review. Kafai and Burke acknowledge this idea in their conceptual paper exploring the shift to a more social view of coding in education, which revolves around the creation and sharing of digital media:

> *Computational thinking should really be thought of as computational participation to emphasize that 'objects-to-think-with'* [– to use one of Papert's key ideas – are indeed] *'objects-to-share-with'* others.

> (Kafai and Burke, 2013, p5)

Activity

Compare these two scenarios, in which young inventors have a definite sense of agency about their work. Can you identify three possible sources of motivation and think of three strategies you would use to create a similar 'can do' ethos in your own classroom?

Wired.co.uk spoke to three boys, Joshua, Ollie and Rory – aged 10, 11 and 10, respectively – who were far too busy building a light sensor for their potential space station to give up much of their time to our frankly unimportant website. 'Look,' said Joshua sternly, 'we're dealing with some fairly major underlying structural instabilities right now.' Oh dear, what was the matter? 'Well it's gone through several redesigns because we wanted to increase the radius of the light sensor using this tinfoil and a pen. It worked,' Joshua demonstrated that the reading on his sensor had indeed increased, 'but it won't stay in place because the hole is too big now.' Ollie looked at Joshua before staring at a table tennis ball. 'I'm not sure why we're using this,' he said. 'For its aesthetics,' replied Joshua, 'It doesn't always have to be about engineering.' Rory was too engrossed with fixing their contraption to give a comment.
(**www.wired.co.uk/news/archive/2013-10/22/next-generation-workshops**)

Raul used Scratch to program an interactive game in his after-school centre. He created the graphics and basic actions for the game but didn't know how to keep score. So when a researcher on our team visited the centre, Raul asked him for help. The researcher showed Raul how to create a variable in Scratch, and Raul immediately saw how he could use it for keeping score. He began playing with the blocks for incrementing variables, then reached out and shook the researcher's hand, saying 'Thank you, thank you, thank you.' The researcher wondered: How many eighth grade algebra teachers get thanked by their students for teaching them about variables?
(**http://web.media.mit.edu/~mres/papers/educational-technology-2012.pdf**)

Learning vs applying

In this set of lessons we focused on applying computational thinking skills to solve a problem rather than just following a step guide to learning a piece of coding syntax. The idea of making decisions and choices is important; there should be scope for creativity in programming projects rather than simply copying worked solutions or following a set of exercises.

While recognising that learning becomes most interesting when children find and solve their own problems, we need to make sure we teach the specific computing skills they need for each area of challenge. Programming involves a complex set of skills, and you will need to balance learning new strategies with applying them. There is a place for guides, examples and tutorials alongside the more open-ended challenges, and we need to make sure to provide activities that are sufficiently scaffolded to ensure that children can succeed. Give children a completely open challenge in Scratch and they are likely to hit problems. Teach the skills relevant to your theme over a number of weeks and you are more likely to end up with successful projects when children develop their own ideas.

For example, in order to make sure that children have the relevant skills at hand, you might spend some time playing and recording audio, and pairing sprites with sounds before designing a musical instrument. You might learn how to write scripts to control movement before designing a robot challenge. Similarly, you could look at the broadcast and speech blocks before making interactive stories, and it would be useful to develop strategies for controlling sprites and adding score variables before inventing games.

Another important aspect of your teaching role is to make relevant computational thinking concepts explicit as children go about their making and inventing. You will need to look for opportunities to tease out the programming concepts from a number of situations, some of which might be completely 'unplugged' and not involve any technology at all. For example, you can compare the use of loops in a knitting pattern or planes waiting to land with the way loops are used in a Scratch project. Or you could liken the use of 'when ... if' conditional statements by a room thermostat adjusting temperature to the use of conditionals in a game to hide a sprite when it touches a red-coloured enemy. You can find a useful summary of key computational concepts and practices on page 8 of the Scratch Curriculum Guide from the ScratchEd Team (Brennan *et al.*, 2011) (Table 5.1).

Table 5.1 Computational concepts and practices

Computational concepts

Concept	Description
sequence	identifying a series of steps for a task
loops	running the same sequence multiple times
parallelism	making things happen at the same time
events	one thing causing another thing to happen
conditionals	making decisions based on conditions
operators	support for mathematical and logical expressions
data	storing, retrieving and updating values

Computational practices

Practice	Description
being iterative and incremental	developing a little bit, then trying it out, then developing some more
testing and debugging	making sure that things work – and finding and fixing mistakes

reusing and remixing	making something by building on what others – or you – have done
abstracting and modularising	building something large by putting together collections of smaller parts

http://scratched.media.mit.edu/resources/scratch-curriculum-guide-draft

By making these concepts and practices explicit you are helping to embed broader logical thinking concepts and a systematic approach to problem solving. This will make it much easier for students to make the transition from working with visual block code in tools such as Scratch to creating written code in languages such as Python, where the logic principles are much the same. In applying their computational thinking skills to different contexts, including iPad apps and puzzles, playground and PE activities, game designing and robotics, children are learning ways of working that are not programming-specific but are transferable to new environments, including applications outside the world of computer science. In this way, you will be using coding not only as an expressive medium but to build understanding of the world. As Miles Berry noted at BETT 2014, computational thinking in this broader sense deserves a place on the curriculum as it *provides unique insights into how the world, natural, technological and social, is, and furthers the scope for students' creative expression* (Berry, 2014).

Real-world links

The physical computing approach outlined in this chapter makes it easier to link programming to real-world scenarios by enabling children to see how their activities relate to objects around them. You can encourage children to think about the pivotal role that control technology plays in our daily lives and discuss how the many digital devices around us work. It is important to get across the idea that the term 'digital' refers to the way in which information is converted to numbers so that computers can interpret it. An unplugged activity based on understanding binary numbers via a row of children holding laminated cards is an effective way of simplifying computers as showing that computers are machines that store information by switching binary digits on and off. You can find some video examples of this activity on Computer Science Unplugged (**http://csunplugged.org/binary-numbers**). Alongside this, another way of demystifying the inner workings of the computer is to use the Raspberry Pi to help children build a mental picture of what is going on inside the box. Building understanding of how digital technology works in this way empowers your pupils to feel that technology is something they can understand and control.

Making it work

In order to turn your classroom into an environment where children use technology to find and explore problems, and invent and make gadgets, you will need to teach them strategies for helping each other. You might begin by modelling that you don't have all the answers and show how you cope when you need to find out how to do something. Some useful strategies are to use blogs and forums on the internet and to access the Help within the software. Try making a working wall with online stickies using a tool such as Padlet (**http://padlet.com**) so that pupils can share strategies. You might give out question tokens, perhaps three per lesson, and encourage children to use them wisely to access your help. Limiting access to the teacher will encourage your pupils to persevere with problems and put more thought into their questions rather than ask lots of 'lazy questions'. It will prompt them to solve problems together and allow you to concentrate on those children who really need your input. Many schools are finding that it can be useful to set up a group of digital leaders (**www.digitalleadernetwork.co.uk**) to support the introduction of computing.

Talk is also crucial to the success of this type of learning as it enables children to make meaning together. This can be facilitated by spending time developing talk skills so that children know how to use talk productively and empathise and listen well. Time also needs to be set aside for discussing and modelling teamwork strategies, such as decision making, assigning roles, giving feedback and managing time. In doing this, children are gaining skills that will be valuable in any workplace. Once again, the teacher is not necessarily an expert programmer but an expert learner, modelling effective learning strategies and knowing when and how much to intervene so that learners are scaffolded to think for themselves and work collaboratively rather than be given answers.

Rossendale School in West Dulwich (Atkins and Hopkin, 2013) provides one example of this approach in action. They embed learning agreements into their teaching and use project briefs to outline the learning content, but put children in charge of defining their own questions. This approach to learning and thinking is based on John Dewey's ideas of children as active learners and the teacher as a facilitator and guide: *The children design products, evaluate outcomes, iteratively improve their creations and publish their findings for others to critique* (Atkins and Hopkin, 2013). This resonates with a design-based learning approach to computing which stresses audience, purpose and product, and the importance of finding generative topics that really engage children and allow them to take ownership of their learning journeys (Brennan *et al.*, 2011).

Activity

How are you going to make the introduction of computing work smoothly in your classroom? Make your own version of Figure 5.3 to show what might work for you.

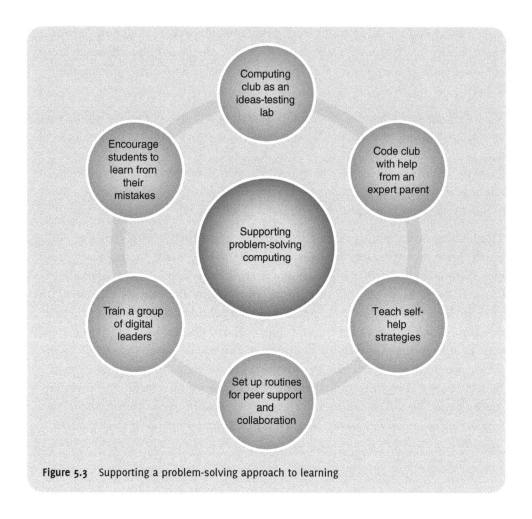

Figure 5.3 Supporting a problem-solving approach to learning

Reflective questions

- Can you come up with a simple explanation of how a computer works?

- Can you think of three real-world scenarios that provide examples of the application of practical computing skills?

- Can you think of an example from your own practice that allowed your pupils to develop ownership of a problem?

Summary

The activities in this chapter are based on the idea that, rather than just teaching a discrete set of coding skills, we are aiming to build opportunities for children to want to program for a purpose. One way of doing this is to use technology to help them explore and affect the world around them. We have considered how providing opportunities for children to tinker with technology helps to build understanding of how it works and empowers them to feel in control of an increasingly digitised world.

We have suggested a number of ways for interacting with the physical world through sensors, motors and robots, and looked at how making these kinds of connections can open up possibilities for applying programming skills. Finally, we thought about how learning to apply computational concepts and practices across a range of situations might lead to new ways of thinking and learning, and we emphasised the importance of social participation when learning to code.

Think about how a pupil-centred approach such as this fits with your own ideas for a scheme of work. Does your planning take into account the fact that pupils may learn more when they make things to show others and gain satisfaction that comes from building and refining their own products and from documenting this process? Look out for practical, creative projects children can work on together and aim to link to their own interests and enthusiasms, and to curriculum topics you are already immersed in. Find a purpose and an audience, and you are well on the way to making learning authentic and meaningful in your classroom. By focusing on the *intellectual adventure* rather than on the teaching of discrete coding skills, says Tom Crick (2012), we will *spread the joy, awe and power of computer science, aiming to make computational thinking (truly a 21st century skill) commonplace.*

Useful links

Code Club: **www.codeclub.org.uk**

A national network of coding clubs run in schools.

CoderDojo: **http://coderdojo.com**

A global collaboration providing free and open learning to young people, especially in programming technology.

Computing At School: **www.computingatschool.org.uk/www.computingatschools.org.uk**

An organisation promoting the teaching of computing in schools, including a wealth of resources.

Craft Computer Club: **www.inpractice.org/2013/08/14/craft-computer-club**

Combining computing skills with craft ideas to run a craft computer club.

Geek Gurl Diaries: **www.geekgurldiaries.co.uk**

An online space launched by ICT teacher Carrie Anne Philbin for young women to learn science and technology skills and to facilitate them to become young technicians and makers.

Making thinking happen: **www.agencybydesign.org/http://makingthinkinghappen.wordpress.com**

The blog space of the Agency by Design project, exploring ideas at the intersection of the maker movement, design thinking and Project Zero frameworks at the Harvard Graduate School of Education.

Mitch Resnick: Let's teach kids to code: **www.ted.com/talks/mitch_resnick_let_s_teach_kids_to_code.html**

One of the inventors of Scratch demonstrates how coding opens up new opportunities for learning.

Raspberry Pi Kid: **http://raspberrypikid.wordpress.com**

A blog about an 11-year-old girl's adventures programming a Raspberry Pi and Lego Mindstorms, which has had over 53,000 views.

STEM Ambassadors Programme: **www.stemnet.org.uk/content/stem-ambassadors**

Recruits people with a background in science, technology, engineering and mathematics (STEM) to volunteer in schools. By contacting the programme you can request a volunteer to help with technical projects in your school.

Further reading

Atkins, K and Hopkin, N (2012) *How We Learn What We Learn.* Available online at: **http://issuu.com/rosendale/docs/how_we_learn** (accessed 24 October 2016).

An account of the thinking that underpins the pedagogy informing a twenty-first-century approach to learning at Rosendale School, West Dulwich, drawing upon ideas from the major learning theorists and international practice.

McManus, S and Cook, M (2013) *Raspberry Pi for Dummies.* Hoboken, NJ: Wiley.

Includes ten inspiring projects for programming in Scratch and Python.

Philbin, C (2013) *Adventures in Raspberry Pi.* West Sussex: Wiley.

Nine fun projects for learning basic programming for Raspberry Pi beginners, each with an accompanying video.

Resnick, M (2012) Point of view: reviving Papert's dream. *Educational Technology*, 52 (4), 42–6.

Reviews how some aspects of Papert's vision from the 1970s for how computing would transform how children learn and play have been fulfilled and suggests that children still need to learn to 'write' as well as 'read' new technologies if they are to achieve the digital fluency that Papert had in mind.

Roque, R (2012) *Making Together: Creative Collaboration for Everyone.* Available online at: **http://llk.media.mit.edu/papers/ricarose-thesis.pdf** (accessed 24 October 2016).

A thesis exploring how we can design learning environments to support the process of creative collaboration on the construction of digital artefacts using a design-based learning approach.

References

Atkins, K and Hopkin, N (2013) *How We Learn What We Learn.* Available online at: **http://issuu.com/ rosendale/docs/how_we_learn** (accessed 24 October 2016).

Berry, M (2014) *More to Computing than Coding ... Presentation at Mirandamod BETT 2014.* Available online at: **http://milesberry.net/2014/01/more-to-computing-than-coding** (accessed 24 October 2016).

Brennan, K and Resnick, M (2012) *Using artifact-based interviews to study the development of computational thinking in interactive media design.* Paper presented at annual American Educational Research Association meeting, Vancouver, BC, Canada.

Brennan, K, Chung, M and Hawson, J (2011) *Creative Computing: A Design-Based Introduction to Computational Thinking.* Available online at: **scratched.gse.harvard.edu/guide/files/ CreativeComputing20140806.pdf** (accessed 24 October 2016).

Crick, T (2012) *Computational Thinking and Thinking About Computing.* Available online at: **http:// drtomcrick.com/2012/06/17/computational-thinking-and-thinking-about-computing** (accessed 24 October 2016).

Kafai, YB and Burke, Q (2013) *The Social Turn in K-12 Programming: Moving from Computational Thinking to Computational Participation.* Available online at: **www.researchgate.net/publication/266653559_ The_social_turn_in_K-12_programming_Moving_from_computational_thinking_to_ computational_participation** (accessed 24 October 2016).

Kenyon, T (2013) *Computing in Schools: Teaching the Next Generation of Computer Scientists.* Available online at: **www.theguardian.com/teacher-network/teacher-blog/2013/feb/13/computer-science-teaching- next-generation** (accessed 24 October 2016).

Papert, S (1980) *Mindstorms: Children, Computers, and Powerful Ideas.* New York: Basic Books.

Papert, S (1993) *The Children's Machine: Rethinking School in the Age of the Computer.* New York: Basic Books.

Resnick, M (2012) Reviving Papert's dream. *Educational Technology*, 52: 42–6.

Upton, E (2012) *How to Summon Your Child's Inner Coder: 10 Questions with Raspberry Pi Inventor Eben Upton.* Available online at: **www.wired.com/business/2012/08/eben-upton** (accessed 24 October 2016).

Chapter 6

Understanding computer networks in KS2

apply underlying principles to understand real-world systems

Learning outcomes

This chapter looks at how to develop pupils' understanding of computer networks and how they provide opportunities for communication and collaboration.

By the end of this chapter you should be able to:

- develop a basic understanding of key computer network terms and practices;
- develop an awareness of ways of developing pupils' knowledge and understanding about computer networks and services;
- develop enthusiasm for pupils to find out more about networks and digital communication infrastructure.

Teachers' Standards

Working through this chapter will help you meet the following standards:

3a. Have a secure knowledge of the relevant subject(s) and curriculum areas, foster and maintain pupils' interest in the subject and address misunderstandings.
4a. Impart knowledge and develop understanding through effective use of lesson time.
4b. Promote a love of learning and children's intellectual curiosity.
6a. Know and understand how to assess the relevant subject and curriculum areas, including statutory assessment requirements.

Links to the National Curriculum

National Curriculum 2014, Computing Programme of Study, KS2 Subject Content

Pupils should learn to:

- understand computer networks, including the internet; how they can provide multiple services, such as the world wide web; and the opportunities they offer for communication and collaboration.

Introduction

So, how do we access information using the internet? How do web pages and e-mails 'miraculously' end up on our computer? A key feature of children's computing skills and digital literacy is developing understanding of digital communication infrastructures that we take for granted on a daily basis. If children understand that all digital communication is enabled and stored on physical devices somewhere within the global network of networks, it is hoped that they can appreciate the need for careful and considered online communication. Developing children's understanding of how we communicate using computer networks is the focus of this chapter.

The chapter focuses on a lesson idea that considers the concept of how data is transmitted and received across the internet. It demystifies the difference between a client and a server, the meaning of acronyms and terms such as ISP, TCP, packets and IP, and how data storage devices work. Next steps will explore how children can be helped to gain insight into HTML through modelling existing pages and using HTML editors.

Lesson idea

The lesson outlined below is an introduction to developing understanding of how we are able to use the internet to access and send information. The lesson is intended to be used with children in Years 4, 5 or 6 and could either be delivered as a standalone lesson or as part of a curriculum theme focused on information sharing and communicating. The lesson will be part of a number of approaches and lessons that will look at how computer networks work – it will be important to ensure that children understand that the internet is only one example of a range of computer networks. It is also important that children realise that the world wide web is only one of a number of services that uses the internet.

The lesson includes a number of 'unplugged' activities – digital devices will not be used, thus enabling children and teachers to reflect on digital activities and place them within familiar physical contexts.

Things you need

- access to YouTube and ability to show to the class the YouTube short film, *There and Back Again: A Packet's Tale – How does the Internet work?* (**http://youtu.be/WwyJGzZmBe8**);
- plastic or cardboard boxes in various large sizes (these are your internet hubs);
- two main types of rope;
- small envelopes;

- sticky notes;

- a range of coloured markers or felt tip pens.

Before you start

It would be useful to have an overview of how networks and the internet work. Please read this as well as the glossary at the end of this chapter. Also watch the YouTube short film: *There and Back Again: A Packet's Tale – How does the Internet work?* (**http://youtu.be/WwyJGzZmBe8**). This gives a basic and clear overview of how web pages are requested and sent via the internet.

Context

Children will have some understanding of what the term 'computer networks' means. To ensure that children have a purpose and 'real' context it would be good to include this lesson within a theme focusing on how we share information and communicate digitally. It will be important to use examples of websites that children regularly use as part of the lesson. Ideally the lesson could be part of a themed morning or afternoon looking at the internet – this 'unplugged' lesson could then be integrated with other computer-based work focusing on researching the location of websites and gaining information about the digital 'journeys' our web use entails.

Learning outcomes for this lesson

Pupils will:

- know basic information about the internet and how information is sent and received;

- be able to explain how information is sent and received using the internet.

Lesson outline

Table 6.1 Lesson planning

Lesson sequence	Grouping and organisation	Suggested resources
Starter/warm-up	Small groups of three or four	Mini-whiteboards A2 poster paper Sticky notes Markers/felt tips

(Continued)

Table 6.1   (Continued)

Lesson sequence	Grouping and organisation	Suggested resources
Main lesson	Whole class (in a large space inside or outside)	Small envelopes Sticky notes Two different types of rope Large cardboard or plastic boxes Router pictures (optional) Mini-whiteboard for teacher use
Summary/plenary	Small groups of three or four	Sticky notes A3 paper Visualiser or means of screencasting work

Starter/warm-up

Divide the class into small groups of three or four. Then get the groups to think of key internet words that they know. Give them a minute to record on mini-whiteboards as many words as they can recall. At this point link to any previous work or discussion about the internet, especially if you have discussed any ideas about how they connect to the internet at home. As a whole class, focus discussion on different types of networks including ISPs and international networks, and quickly record as many words as possible. As this is being recorded, try and focus on the key words that will be used in the main part of the lesson – you may need to add your own focus words at this point.

Following this, get the children to work in pairs to create a diagram of how they understand computer networks. Using sticky notes, A2 poster paper and/or mini-whiteboards, the children will explore how they think computer networks work. This will build on a previous session that focused on developing understanding of computer networks – including wireless and wired home networks.

This activity should take about five or ten minutes and will give you an understanding of how much children have recalled and understood networks. As the activity develops, challenge misconceptions and promote development of knowledge, such as how computer networks link to each other. This will give opportunities to introduce some of the key terms which will be used in the main part of the lesson (routers, ISP, hub, IP addresses).

Main lesson

This part of the lesson will need to be in a fairly large open space such as a school hall or outside in the playground (the playground is ideal, as it gives the chance to label and annotate using chalk).

Before moving to the open space, show pupils the YouTube short film: *There and Back Again: A Packet's Tale – How does the Internet work?* (**http://youtu.be/ WwyJGzZmBe8**). Explain to the children that they are going to make their own 'internet' and physically move as packets of data to deliver web pages.

After moving with the children to the large space, show them the range of equipment you are going to use. Get them to think about what the equipment will be used for: boxes for servers and routers; ropes for wire and cable connections; envelopes to act as data packets.

Now divide the class into groups of about 12–15 (the number will vary depending on how you allocate their roles). Then allocate children to these different roles:

- computer software: two children – these children will write the data packets (on envelopes: one to request the website/multiple for the incoming message). They will also ensure that the data packets are in the right format when they receive them – if they aren't, they could shout, 'Can't read this!'

- IP address allocators: two children – these children will allocate the outgoing and incoming IP addresses;

- router/server disruptors: two children – one child on each side will keep changing which routers can and cannot be used; a cone or something similar will signify when a router is out of use;

- cabling engineers: four children – these children will ensure that the cabling is maintained and connected;

- outgoing data packet: one child – this child will deliver the outgoing request to the web server;

- incoming data packets: four or five children – these children will deliver the data packets along different routes to the recipient's computer.

Get the children to work out, using their allocated roles and the equipment provided, how they are going to recreate the journey of the request and delivery of a web page. At this point provide a written description of the format of a data packet – ensure that children recreate this when they write envelopes to deliver between the incoming and outgoing computers.

You will have decided how to show the data packet format before this stage. You may also have decided on the format of IP address that you would like the children to write – ideally, some randomisation would be good; using dice would be an easy way of achieving this. However, children will quickly find out that randomising all the IP address will take too long, therefore certain sections could stay the same.

Run through this activity a number of times. Reallocate roles to children each time; get them to experience a number of roles.

Commentary

Your challenge will be to ensure that this activity is at a fast pace. IP allocation and writing the data packets could slow down the pace, as could decisions made on router problems and how 'computers' send and receive the data packets.

Summary/plenary

An essential part of this lesson will be finding out how the children have developed an understanding of some of the main networking concepts and ideas. An ideal activity would be to give small groups of children pieces of A3 'sugar' or poster paper and get them to draw and record how we request and receive web pages (if children have access to a digital device they could record their ideas using mind or concept-mapping software and/or apps). This would then create an immediate symbolic representation of the concrete task that they carried out in the main part of the lesson.

Critical questions to ask pupils:

- In what format do we send and receive messages (hopefully getting some recall of packets and packet formats)?

- What role do routers play in 'channelling' messages?

- Are there main centres for 'routing' messages between countries?

Displaying these on a class working wall (either physically or digitally) would enable children and adults to revisit ideas over the next few days. Children could add or edit their ideas, especially if they have been able to do further research at home or school.

Taking it further

We have had a more detailed look at a lesson plan for just one area of the Programme of Study which looks at developing understanding of computer networks. Before this lesson it would be good to get children to have an overall understanding of how familiar computers at home or school communicate with other networks.

A Prezi discussion on the computing planning site **http://code-it.co.uk/csplanning. html** gives an ideal simplified overview of networks, routers and internet service providers. Children could then be asked to draw a pictorial/symbolic overview of the computer networks they use; this would only require large paper, coloured pens/pencils and possibly sticky notes. This task works particularly well in pairs or threes, where children can draw multiple networks, ideally with different ISPs. During this session it would also be good to show children the schematic map of a representation of internet links, available at **http://internet-map.net**.

Following the main lesson of focus in this chapter, it would be interesting to quickly revisit children's ideas about how we send and receive messages using the internet. Ideally, the physical or digital posters that they created in the plenary could be displayed after the lesson. Children could then revisit these, and this would present an opportunity for further discussion.

After gaining some basic knowledge and understanding of network infrastructure, children could then develop understanding of finding the location of websites and servers across the world. There are a number of websites that convert web addresses into IP addresses, such as **www.getip.com**. There are also a number of other websites that can find out the location of IP addresses.

Children could also develop understanding of hypertext markup language (HTML). This would allow them to understand the need for a common language for web pages to work across the internet. There are a number of engaging free resources online, such as Mozilla Thimble (**https://thimble.webmaker. org**) or Webmaker (**https://webmaker.org/en-US**). These could be used for classroom activities for pupils to gain basic understanding of web conventions and standardisation.

Activity

Ideally a number of areas of the Computing Programme of Study should be embedded within other curriculum areas. Think of which subjects, topics or themes could easily work with the lesson that has been presented. Could the activities focus on particular websites and resources used within these topics or subjects?

Discussion

Why learn about computer networks?

Dido Harding, the chief executive officer of TalkTalk, during an interview on BBC Radio 4 *Woman's Hour* (5 November 2013), pointed to the need for children to gain much more knowledge about networks and the internet. She used the analogy of road safety sessions and adverts that were common in the 1970s and 1980s to call for the *road safety skills of today*, where children gain knowledge of the internet, its main routes and structures and its potential areas of harm.

Certainly, children are spending an increasing amount of time using the internet (Ofcom, 2012). However, it is probable that their understanding of the way in which they are sending and receiving messages and information is not growing at the same rate. Many internet safety approaches (**www.thinkuknow.co.uk, http://ceop.police. uk**) call for educational professionals and parents to develop children's awareness of the internet. This may include developing understanding of how search engines work. However, these approaches do not develop detailed knowledge of how networks work, how data is stored and how we access data using networks. With this type of information children may consider the need to think of where they are storing data. They might also understand that images and video are stored in a physical location and can easily be copied and stored elsewhere.

One of the reasons for the development of this Computing Programme of Study included reference to the need to meet the professional imperative of developing digital and computing literacy. In one of its curriculum update documents, the British Computer Society Academy of Computing (2012) stated, *We also need professionals capable of protecting our information, our digital infrastructure and our intellectual property. The path to this professionalism can only begin in schools* (p14). The need to develop pupils' awareness of the structure and workings of a network is a significant element of this approach. Developing this understanding enables children to be aware of the context of the development of programming and code. Awareness of how messages are sent and received through routers and between servers allows children to realise that standardisation and being precise are essential when using conventions and code for communication software.

Demystifying the internet

An important reason for developing children's understanding of network is to attempt to demystify the entity that we refer to as the internet. This network of networks is known by a number of nouns, including the web, the net, the information superhighway, cyberspace and also perhaps the cloud. When discussing the internet with children, they commonly refer to e-mail or websites and sometimes include names of websites, such as Google, Amazon or Facebook. However, their response broadens out when some of the activities discussed previously are undertaken. They also quickly develop a desire to find out where information is stored.

Chapter 7 focuses specifically on developing information-searching skills. This is obviously a core part of developing information literacy. However, if children are also given the opportunity to develop a basic understanding of how network infrastructure works, they will soon develop a sense that all information is stored on a server somewhere. This will allow children to realise that they may need to be systematic in the way they search for information. Being systematic is integrally related to understanding that search engines are merely searching across a very wide range of servers and caches of information.

As knowledge and understanding develop it is then possible to engage pupils with more discerning discussions about the quality and provenance of information. Understanding that data is stored on a server somewhere in the world and that they may be able to trace this allows further questions to develop. Common questions are about who has created this data, why they have created it and for what purpose.

Reflective questions

- How will you ensure that you are able to differentiate a lesson of this nature? What methods could you use to support all types of learners?

- How could you use children to lead and facilitate some of the activities during the lesson?

- How could homework activities be used to develop understanding further?

Summary

This chapter focused on developing basic understanding and knowledge about computer networks. It allows children to investigate how we request and receive information using networks, servers and routers. A common theme within this book is the use of 'unplugged' activities within computing lessons. The intention is that this is combined with further child-led activities searching for further information and investigating network structures, thus widening understanding of difficult concepts but with some initial 'real-world' experience.

This is the first primary Programme of Study that contains direction to develop this type of knowledge and skills about network technologies. Developing knowledge about the infrastructure of networks and networking should be seen as an important accompaniment to other areas that focus on developing algorithms and debugging programs. Context is again important in that children can begin to understand the need for standardised and systematic approaches when using digital technologies. If children realise that a web page they are viewing may have been requested from a web server thousands of miles away they may develop a better understanding of the complexities of the internet. Children should then realise the need for some standard way of writing computer code to allow all routers and technologies to process this information.

This area of the Computing Programme of Study could easily be neglected by teachers as they may feel that they do not have sufficient personal knowledge and understanding. Hopefully this chapter, including links to resources and a glossary, should enable all teachers, with different levels of technological experience, to attempt engaging lessons and discussions.

Useful links

http://code-it.co.uk

http://computer.howstuffworks.com/internet/basics/question549.htm

http://computer.howstuffworks.com/web-server2.htm

Further reading

Naace/CAS Curriculum Guidance. Available online at: **http://goo.gl/GH95V7** (accessed 20 December 2016).

References

BCS Academy of Computing (2012) *Computing in the National Curriculum for Schools, Update of Activities.* Available online at: **http://academy.bcs.org/sites/academy.bcs.org/files/national-curriculum-schools.pdf** (accessed 20 December 2016).

Ofcom (2012) *Children and Parents: Media Use and Attitudes Report.* London: Ofcom.

Glossary

HTML – hypertext markup language is the main language for creating web pages that can be displayed in a web browser. HTML is a set of information which categorises text and other artefacts using tags enclosed within angle brackets < >.

IP (internet protocol) address – each computer on a network has its own unique address (like a house or flat address). This helps data packets to get from and to the right destination. Most computers have an IP address which is changed frequently by the network provider. If you go to **www.123myip.co.uk** this will tell you your current IP address.

ISP – an internet service provider is a company, such as BT, TalkTalk, Virgin or Sky, that allows our home computers to access the internet.

packets – any e-mails or web pages that are sent or received are usually made up of a series of packets of information. Each packet has a number of types of information to make sure the packet gets where it needs to go and manages to get back, together with the other packets which make up the overall e-mail or web page. The packet usually has:

- the sender's IP address;
- the IP address of where the packet is going;
- information on how many packets the message/web page has been broken up into;
- something to tell which packet this is in the overall message/web page.

routers – when data packets are sent or received between different computer networks they pass through a router. The router 'reads' the address information and makes sure the packet gets to the right destination. Routers come in different sizes depending on the amount of 'traffic' of packets that they process. At home we are familiar with our routers that allow our computers and digital devices to access the internet and link us to our ISP. ISPs have much bigger routers to 'route' data from many sources.

TCP/IP (transmission control protocol/internet protocol) – when a computer is connected to the internet it uses a common language or protocol. All computers use this code. This code specifies how data is formatted, addressed, transmitted, routed and received at the destination.

website servers – these are computers which physically store the files and code which make up the web page or pages (which we often call a website) you are looking for. This YouTube clip tells you how to find out the location of the website servers: **http://youtu.be/T2WoznZaJVE**.

Chapter 7

Searching wisely for digital information in KS2

Adam Scribbans

understand the fundamental principles of information

Learning outcomes

This chapter will allow you to achieve the following outcomes, as outlined in the Computing Programme of Study.

By the end of this chapter you should be able to:

- be responsible, competent, confident and creative users of information and communication technology.

Key Stage 1

- use technology safely and respectfully, keeping personal information private; identify where to go for help and support when you have concerns about content or contact on the internet or other online technologies.

Key Stage 2

- use search technologies effectively, appreciate how results are selected and ranked, and be discerning in evaluating digital content;
- use technology safely, respectfully and responsibly; recognise acceptable/unacceptable behaviour; identify a range of ways to report concerns about content and contact.

Teachers' Standards

Working through this chapter will help you meet the following standards:

3a. Have a secure knowledge of the relevant subject(s) and curriculum areas, foster and maintain pupils' interest in the subject, and address misunderstandings.

4b. Promote a love of learning and children's intellectual curiosity.

6a. Know and understand how to assess the relevant subject and curriculum areas, including statutory assessment requirements.

Introduction

This chapter looks at how to help children stay safe online, how children can find what they are looking for and what to do if they come across something they shouldn't. Many adults still believe that anything written down by 'them' is always right and always to be believed. Maybe it is a generation thing but often you will hear intelligent and well-educated individuals saying things such as, 'They now say that you should leave your PC on all the time to make it last longer', or 'They have proved that the average person swallows, on average, seven spiders in their sleep per year' or 'Did you see that they have now found an IKEA on Mars?' OK, the last one might be too far-fetched to be believed but you can probably imagine someone saying it – you might even have someone in mind.

In preparing children for the digital age, we have a deep responsibility to ensure that they are prepared for 'them' in all their forms and understand that the ultimate responsibility for children's safety, in both the virtual and real world, is up to them. Just as it is impossible to watch children all the time when they are playing, it is impossible to watch them all the time when they are online. Obviously there is a choice that all parents and guardians have to make: Do I wrap my children up in cotton wool and never let them outside to play, or do I accept that they will grow into adults and allow them to learn responsibility by managing their exposure to risk? As teachers, we unconsciously manage this balance on a daily, even hourly, basis, even in what we ask our pupils to read. We could make everything easy for them but, as we all know, learning occurs most when we are outside our comfort zone.

As teachers, it is imperative that we manage children's experiences in cyberspace, not least because they often know more about it than us. We want them to become citizens of the digital age, but we do not want them to fall victim to unscrupulous 'them'. We could put on, as many schools do, so many layers of protection that pupils will never even come close to inappropriate content, but is this really preparing them for the real world? What happens when they get home or visit friends and have unrestricted access? If we haven't prepared them adequately for the 'dark side' of the web, we have failed them and they will become victims.

It is important that we accept that, although we might hope that parents will guide their children through the dangers of life online, we know this is often not the case. Also, it would be irresponsible for us to leave it to secondary educators, as many preteen children are already 'natives' of the digital world. Whilst the intent is not to scaremonger, it is important that we, as teachers, are aware of some of the very real risks our children are being exposed to online.

In a recent survey, it was found that:

> *One in five respondents in a study of primary pupils claimed to have met someone they had only previously known online.*

A sizeable majority of the children who took the survey were aged between nine and 11 and a significant minority were also regularly awake into the small hours on computers in their bedrooms and were never supervised by their parents.

Almost a fifth said they had never received any training on safe internet usage – and of those who had, 12% said they found the safety lessons to be useless. Many were claiming to be years older online than their true age.

(Kennedy, 2013)

More than half (53 per cent) of parents put the onus on education, saying that knowing their child is learning about e-safety in school would make them feel better equipped to help keep their child stay safe online.

But nearly a third (32 per cent) of parents admit better parental personal knowledge of the internet and social networks would help.

(Roberts, 2013)

Ofcom's report on internet safety measures in December 2015 outlined some key areas to consider. The number of households that have taken up the options available for family-friendly network filtering remains stubbornly low. This clearly raises concern as many children access the internet without supervision (Ofcom report, 2015).

Considering the pace of change these figures represent, the onus is squarely on primary teachers to ensure that the country's children are prepared for whatever is to come in the next few years. With the current proliferation of tablet computers and smartphones, we are already in a position of losing control over what children are exposed to. With no knowing what the next technological revolution will be, we have to make sure we get the message right as early as possible. Who knows what children might be using in ten years' time to access the world wide web – Smart watches? Smart t-shirts? Interactive teddy bears? Social networking pillows?

Lesson idea: teaching online safety

Teaching primary-aged children to be safe online is tricky, just as teaching stranger danger is tricky. Getting the right balance between 'terrifying the life out of them' and 'all adults are warm and cuddly, just like Father Christmas' is not easy. Any teacher who has had a discussion a bit like this will understand:

Teacher: If you are lost, try and find a police officer.

Child: But I don't know any police officers.

Teacher: Policeman. That's OK, you can trust a policeman.

Child: But you just told us not to trust strangers and I told you I don't know any policemen, so they must be strangers.

Even when you try and qualify this with 'Anyone in a uniform is OK', you are opening yourself up to all sorts of issues. How does a child recognise a uniform? Are all people in uniform to be trusted? Is someone coming off a shift at McDonalds to be trusted?

We want children to engage in the digital world they are inheriting, for a truly marvellous place it is. But we also want to instil a sense of discrimination and what used to be called being 'streetwise'; now maybe this should be called 'webwise', as advocated by the BBC, or 'digiwise', or similar. However, being streetwise was never a subject taught at school; it was something you learnt yourself through experience – the 'school of hard knocks'. In reality I don't think any of us would advocate using this approach as a way of ensuring online safety, as the potential for disaster is just too large considering the size of the digital world children have access to from the comfort of their own bedroom. The question is: How do we allow children to learn the hard knocks of life in the web without putting them in mortal and moral danger?

Lesson objectives

Any lesson or series of lessons on online safety has to be, as with any lesson objective, achievable and realistic as well as suitable for the age and abilities you are teaching, with appropriate differentiation. To assume that children will have learnt how to be safe online and disseminate truth from fiction in one lesson is like assuming that they have learnt addition because you taught it last week.

We can start building digital wisdom from an early age through simple games involving finding and correcting errors – just because it is written down doesn't mean it is right. In Key Stage 1 (KS1) this may involve writing a set of instructions (algorithms) with incorrect words, phrases or sequences. These could even be done in a role-play environment, e.g. 'I will give you a set of instructions for getting ready for PE. Can any of you spot where I have gone wrong?'

For KS2, they need to go further than this by actually identifying inaccuracies on the web. A good place to start is by using the site All About Explorers (**www. allaboutexplorers.com),** which was designed specifically for teaching some of the hard knocks that children need to learn before they can safely make full use of the web. The whole site is mostly fiction but presented in a way that can be believed by taking famous explorers and creating fictional biographies.

How you use the site depends on how cruel you want to be. If you really want to let your children learn through experience, there is no reason why you can't present your lessons, not as ICT or computing, but as a history lesson linked to the Tudors, Vikings or Victorians. You could even use it as part of an English lesson on writing a biography or a historical diary entry. Your brighter children may recognise inconsistencies but as long as you maintain the charade there will be plenty of excellent discussion and learning to come out of it. If you don't have a mean streak, the site is still useful for spotting truth and fiction by cross-referencing it against other sites and reference books; you might even want to offer a prize for the individual or team that can evidence the most inaccuracies. This task is easily differentiated through different expectations and approaches. For lower ages and the less able, producing cards for them to match fiction against fact will work very well (Figure 7.1). More ideas and support can be found under 'For Teachers' at this site.

Figure 7.1   Matching fiction against fact

Finding what we want

Being safe online and recognising that not everything out there is truthful is one thing, but finding the best source of information is quite another. Putting in a search string that brings back the right or best sites is not as easy as it sounds and, without care and forethought, the potential for stumbling across inappropriate sites is huge. But children are not just stumbling over inappropriate content; they are actively seeking it out. Combine this with the rise in use of portable devices, often unsupervised, and a worrying trend is emerging.

While Google has come a long way in ensuring online safety, there are always people who will try and get around their safeguards for their own entertainment and many words which would appear innocent can lead to inappropriate images. There are other searches that may lead to misleading or completely inaccurate information. The following website is harmless but totally fictitious: **http://zapatopi.net/treeoctopus.html**. It can be a useful exercise to ask Key Stage 2 children to review it. Many children will initially believe that the information has to be true. On discovering that the website is fictitious, children are likely to become more aware of the need to be discerning when viewing online information.

Major concerns were raised following the Byron Review (2008) into children's lack of knowledge and resilience of the dangers presented by the online world. Amongst its findings was the realisation that children were spending most of their online time unsupervised, for which they had not been prepared. The focus by schools had been to keep them safe within school but there had not been enough recognition of the need to ensure children were aware of the potential dangers and how to stay safe online. Websites such as ThinkUKnow (**www.thinkuknow.co.uk**) produced by Child Exploitation and Online Protection (CEOP) and KnowITAll (**www.childnet.com/resources/know-it-all-for-primary**) have provided lots of support for teachers and resources for schools.

The Ofsted report on e-safety in 2010 recommended that schools:

- *audit the training needs of all staff and provide training to improve their knowledge of and expertise in the safe and appropriate use of new technologies;*

- *work closely with all families to help them ensure that their children use new technologies safely and responsibly both at home and at school;*

- *use pupils' and families' views more often to develop e-safety strategies.*

(Ofsted, 2010)

The key findings in 2015 indicated that online training is being delivered across schools, but the children's interpretation of what online safety means is often unclear. Training was considered inconsistent and not always implemented by staff. Knowledge of reporting inappropriate sites was often unclear to both the schools and pupils.

So, the big question is: How do we let children explore the internet with all its glorious diversity, knowledge and potential while maintaining their innocence and our responsibilities as a teacher?

- Teach children how to make effective multiword key word searches.

- Talk about appropriate and inappropriate content on the web.

- Practise simple routines for dealing with inappropriate content.

- Manage all children's journeys into the digital world. Start with offline computers, move on to 'locked-down' systems, then managed systems, and finally give unrestricted access.

- Ensure your school has an up-to-date e-safety policy that is regularly updated. If it doesn't, you might want to suggest it defines one with some urgency.

- As stated above, e-safety policies are only truly effective when the parents are involved as well. This needs to be something that we all engage in, but it is for the school to manage.

- Should we allow primary-aged children unrestricted access to the internet? Almost definitely, no!

- Do primary-aged children have unrestricted access to the internet? Almost definitely, yes!

- Is it the responsibility of teachers to ensure that children are safe online? Unfortunately, yes!

Any activity associated with school life that has an impact on the wellbeing of a child, whether it occurs in school or out, is the responsibility of the school and its teachers. A prime example of this is cyberbullying, the number one concern of many pre- and post-adolescents. If the bullying is taking place between school peers, it doesn't matter where or when it occurs; as teachers, it is our responsibility.

Multiword searches

Children ask questions – that's what they do.

The internet is a fantastic place to be a child. You can ask it any question you like and it will give you not just one answer but millions of answers: 'triffic!'

Practising searches is the one thing you can do as a teacher to help children remain safe online and find the answers they were looking for. Simple games, worksheets and exercises can quickly turn your pupils from painfully slow-typing dinosaurs into sleek, street-savvy foxes.

In essence, your pupils need to think about the questions they want answered and then become adept at recognising the key words that will make their searches faster and more efficient. For example:

Sally is researching the Vikings and wants to know where they sailed to. Without guidance she may type something like this into the computer:

Where did the vikings sale there ships to?

In doing this, she may take up half the lesson and not get the results she was hoping for, leading to her becoming disengaged with the lesson.

However, with some guidance and preplanning, her question could be more accurate:

What were the first journeys of the Vikings?

Now we are getting closer to asking the right question, but we do not need the full sentence structure for an internet search. Google and other search engines completely ignore common words such as 'what', 'the', 'of' and, by typing them in, all Sally has done is waste valuable ICT time.

~~What were the~~ first journeys ~~of the~~ Vikings?

Now the search comes back with only sites offering information about the first journeys of Vikings, saving time, increasing achievement and speeding up learning.

By teaching children to use multiword searches over single-word searches, we also help them to avoid inappropriate content. While deviants might try and get around online protection by picking innocent words or phrases for their images or site, the chances of them matching a child's multiword search are huge. If a child uses three or more key words, the chances of them stumbling across inappropriate content are reduced exponentially. For example:

One word	bird	(Not all 'birds' are of the feathered variety)
Two words	bird nest	
Three words	bird nest eggs	
We can also shore up their search habits by insisting that they are more specific about their question:		
Four words	robin nest eggs chicks	Lots of images of cute robins in nests, aaah!

The chances of children now finding something they shouldn't are so far removed as to be negligible and if we can get children to do this exercise instinctively, the safer they will be and they will be making much better use of their time. You might want to try it for yourself with this one, although it is not recommended (do not try this with your class):

One word	big or doggy	Innocent enough words you'd think
Two words	big wet	Look if you dare
Three words	big wet doggy	
Four words	big wet doggy swimming	Aaah, look at the funny doggy swimming!

Search operators

While you might not want to introduce search operators in KS1, there is no reason not to in KS2. By using these operators it is possible to narrow the search down as far as you want.

AND
Use *AND* if you want to retrieve references that contain both of the terms you are using. This can narrow a search to find fewer, more relevant, references (Figure 7.2).

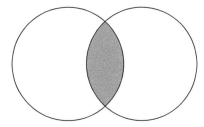

Figure 7.2 Diagram showing *AND* results, e.g. pollution *AND* oil spills

OR
Use *OR* if you want to retrieve references that contain either one of the terms you are using, or both terms together.

This can broaden a search to find more references.

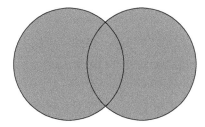

Figure 7.3 Diagram showing *OR* results, e.g. pollution *OR* oil spills

NOT
Use *NOT* if you want to exclude references that contain a particular term. Use with caution!

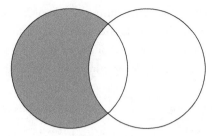

Figure 7.4   Diagram showing *NOT* results, e.g. pollution *NOT* oil spills

Brackets ( )

Also, many databases allow you to use brackets to make more complicated searches. For example:

(pollution OR oil) *AND* seabirds

The brackets indicate the order that the combining of terms is made in.

(www.bristol.ac.uk/library/support/findinginfo/search-terms)

When children do find inappropriate content

It is critical that children are given the tools and strategies necessary for dealing with inappropriate content when, not if, they come across it. For this to be effective we need to give our pupils an understanding of what is, and what is not, appropriate.

No one is suggesting that this should be achieved by showing examples of appropriate and inappropriate images/content but there are some simple steps that we can discuss with our pupils:

1. What is appropriate? Anything that is relevant to our work and age. If it would be allowed on CBeebies and/or CBBC, it is appropriate.

2. What is inappropriate? Anything that is not to do with what we are looking for and not relevant to our work or age; if you wouldn't see it on CBBC, then it is inappropriate.

3. What do we do if we find something we think we shouldn't? Go back and try a different search with better words.

4. What do we do if we come across something that scares or frightens us? Talk to an adult you trust and discuss what you saw.

5. What do we do if we are tempted to look for things we know we shouldn't or our friends tell us to search for something we don't understand or feel comfortable about? Don't! It is important that we all take our safety online seriously. You wouldn't run across a road because your friends told you to, so why would you search for something inappropriate online just because they told you to?

Assessment and progression

As mentioned at the beginning of this chapter, it is essential that this subject is not a 'one-lesson wonder'. Only by constant reinforcement can we ensure that our pupils are adequately prepared for the digital world. Whilst summative assessment is possible through testing, formative and informal assessment offers a much better way of monitoring progress and thus informing future lessons. This assessment can, and should, be conducted whenever your pupils are using a computer to search for resources.

Key assessment opportunities

- Do they prepare their searches beforehand?

- Are they using effective multiword searches?

- If they do not find what they were looking for, how do they refine their search?

- When they find what they are looking for, do they test its accuracy or accept it as correct?

- Are they using just one source of information or are they comparing two or more sites?

By keeping these simple questions in mind, planning for progression becomes easier.

Conclusion

Whilst this chapter focuses on safe searching and online information, it is important to keep in mind all the other threats our children are open to online, including cyberbullying, cyberstalking and online grooming. Our responsibility as teachers now goes beyond the walls of our classrooms, out into a 24-hour, world wide web of possibilities, both good and bad. By accepting the possibilities and real threats that this world offers our pupils, we can really help them to make the most of this amazing opportunity.

Further reading

All About Explorers. Available online at: www.allaboutexplorers.com (accessed 20 December 2016).

Bristol University, How to use search engines effectively: Google and beyond. Available online at: www.bristol.ac.uk/library/support/findinginfo/search-engines (accessed 20 December 2016).

Byron, T (2008) *Safer Children in a Digital World*. Available online at: http://media.education.gov.uk/assets/files/pdf/s/safer%20children%20in%20a%20digital%20world%20the%202008%20byron%20review.pdf (accessed 20 December 2016).

Child Exploitation and Online Protection Centre: internet safety. Available online at: **http://ceop.police. uk** (accessed 20 December 2016).

Get Safe Online. Available online at: **www.getsafeonline.org** (accessed 20 December 2016).

KidSMART. Available online at: **www.kidsmart.org.uk** (accessed 20 December 2016).

Savage, M and Barnett, A (2015) *Digital Literacy for Primary Teachers*. St Albans: Critical Publishing.

UK Council for Child Internet Safety. Available online at: **www.gov.uk/government/policy-advisory-groups/uk-council-for-child-internet-safety-ukccis** (accessed 20 December 2016).

References

Belshaw, D (2012) What is 'digital literacy'? A pragmatic investigation (Doctoral dissertation, Durham University). Available online at: **www.slideshare.net/dajbelshaw/the-essential-elements-of-digital-literacies** (accessed 20 December 2016).

Child Exploitation and Online Protection Centre, ThinkUKnow. Available online at: **www. thinkuknow.co.uk** (accessed 20 December 2016).

Kennedy, M (2013) Children's internet use survey offers warning to parents. *The Guardian*, 21 October, p12.

KnowITAll. Available online at: **www.childnet.com/resources/know-it-all-for-primary** (accessed 20 December 2016).

Ofsted (2010) *The Safe Use of New Technologies*. Available online at: **http://webarchive.nationalarchives. gov.uk/20120408131156/http:/www.ofsted.gov.uk/resources/safe-use-of-new-technologies** (accessed 20 December 2016).

Ofcom (2013) *Children and Parents: Media Use and Attitudes Report*. London: Ofcom.

Ofcom (2015) Ofcom report on internet safety measures. Available online at: **http://stakeholders.ofcom. org.uk/binaries/internet/fourth_internet_safety_report.pdf** (accessed 20 December 2016).

Roberts, L (2013) *Anti-Bullying Alliance Website*. Available online at: **www. anti-bullyingalliance.org. uk/aba-week/highlights-of-2013.aspx** (accessed 20 December 2016).

Chapter 8

Using technology purposefully in KS2

select, use and combine a variety of software (including internet services) on a range of digital devices to design and create a range of programs, systems and content that accomplish given goals, including collecting, analysing, evaluating and presenting data and information

Learning outcomes

By the end of this chapter you should be able to:

- develop an understanding of ways of creating opportunities for children to use technology to produce creative curriculum outcomes;
- design a series of lessons which allow creation and editing of digital content within a range of subjects;
- understand approaches to teaching and learning which enable children to explore their own methods of creating digital content using a range of software applications.

Teachers' Standards

Working through this chapter will help you meet the following standards:

3a. Have a secure knowledge of the relevant subject(s) and curriculum areas, foster and maintain pupils' interest in the subject and address misunderstandings.
4a. Impart knowledge and develop understanding through effective use of lesson time.
4b. Promote a love of learning and children's intellectual curiosity.
6a. Know and understand how to assess the relevant subject and curriculum areas, including statutory assessment requirements.

> ### Links to the National Curriculum
>
> *Links to the National Curriculum 2014, Computing Programme of Study, KS2 Subject Content*
>
> Pupils should learn to:
>
> - select, use and combine a variety of software (including internet services) on a range of digital devices to design and create a range of programs, systems and content that accomplish given goals, including collecting, analysing, evaluating and presenting data and information.

Introduction

This chapter will consider opportunities for Key Stage 2 children to produce creative digital outcomes using a range of software applications. The lesson idea attempts to centre the use of technology within a curriculum idea that meets objectives from a number of different subjects. The discussion section explores the term 'digital literacy' and provides comment and overview on a range of applications and approaches to the creative use of technology across the curriculum.

Lesson idea

These ideas will lead to the development of a thematic set of lessons covering objectives in English, science and geography. In these lessons children will be asked to design, write and present short weather forecasts using a range of software and technologies.

Things you need

- access to laptops, desktops and/or tablets;

- www.metoffice.gov.uk/education/teachers;

- www.metoffice.gov.uk/education/kids/weather-diary;

- www.metlink.org/weather-climate-resources-children/key-stages-weather-climate/key-stage-2-weather.html;

- www.kudlian.net/products/icanpresent/Home.html.

Before you start

This lesson idea embeds the use of technology into the learning outcomes for English and geography. Careful consideration will be needed in relation to where this lesson idea fits into the medium- and long-term planning for all three curriculum areas.

Children will need to work in groups for planning, research and production, so it is important to plan these groups. Mixed ability would work best as the more literate may support the children who are more challenged by literacy. A mixed-ability balance in terms of creativity and technological abilities would also support children who find these aspects more difficult. It is important to remember that the most literate will not necessarily have creative and technical strengths. The aim would be to provide groups with complementary abilities.

Context

This set of lessons will assume that you have developed some desire and motivation to use technology in flexible and purposeful ways. It may be useful to look first at the discussion section of this chapter, as this will provide a good orientation about this style of approach. This discussion outlines the range of applications, both desktop/laptop- and tablet-based, which allow children to use technology to develop, combine and refine their ideas.

Learning outcomes for this set of lessons

English:

- understanding the use of different vocabulary for specific purposes;
- features of script writing;
- writing for different audiences;
- speaking for a specific audience.

Geography:

- locational knowledge:
  - o name and locate counties and cities of the United Kingdom, geographical regions and their identifying human and physical characteristics, key topographical features (including hills, mountains, coasts and rivers).
- human and physical geography:
  - o describe and understand key aspects of physical geography, including: climate zones, biomes and vegetation belts, rivers, mountains, volcanoes and earthquakes, and the water cycle.

Lesson outline

These ideas could be developed into a range of ways of designing and delivering lessons. Ideally they would be best developed as a unit of work within English, focusing on speaking and listening skills, including script writing and analysis of different types of television programmes. An approach of this nature would ideally involve a series of activities blocked within a few days or over a week. These activities would include distinct English lessons, but then also include preparation time to develop and present the final product.

The discussion within this chapter refers to the process of plan–research–produce, aimed at developing digital artefacts allowing children to express their learning in creative ways. The discussion in Chapter 3, which looks at manipulating digital content in KS1, refers to an information-processing approach of inputs–processes–outcomes. This process again assumes the production of creative digital outcomes (digital artefacts).

Similar processes will need to be considered when deciding how to design the learning activities for this lesson idea. Children will need to have access to a range of digital resources and tools, which will enable them to explore and consolidate their ideas. These resources and tools may be already familiar to the children; however, there may also be a need to have ICT skills sessions during the learning activities.

Plan and research

An initial task will be to watch, discuss and analyse weather forecasts. These can be accessed in a range of ways, perhaps using weather websites (**www.metoffice.gov. uk, www.metcheck.com, www.accuweather.com**). Children should have the chance to search for weather websites as well as weather broadcasts either designed for radio or television. The overall digital outcome for this unit of work is to produce a weather forecast video; therefore it will be essential for children to watch a number of weather forecasts that are easily available through the websites of a range of UK news organisations.

An initial English focus would be to analyse the nature of the language used during forecasts. Does the language differ between forecasts from different organisations? Is the language designed to convey messages in a certain way? What are the common terms used in forecasts – could a weather word bank be easily created? The discussion refers to a number of digital tools that will enable children to record and manipulate ideas.

During this phase of planning and research, children will need to recap the main features of script writing and writing text for video presentation. This will probably require another distinct English lesson focused on this particular genre. Part of the discussion and analysis will look at the style of language used within scripts. At this stage, it would be useful to become familiar with the digital autocue tool that you are going to use for the weather forecast video.

There are a number of tools that could be used, such as CuePrompter (**www. cueprompter.com**), tools built into software such as I Can Present or a number of tablet apps, such as Teleprompter Pro Lite. This will allow children to develop awareness of the way in which an autocue works and how this may impact on the text they will produce for their script. Layout, syntax, sentence length and vocabulary will all be considerations. At this stage children could ensure that they introduce weather vocabulary and weather forecast script features into the text they produce when they are 'practising' with the software.

Commentary

When planning and delivering a project of this nature it is important to balance ICT skills delivery and experience carefully alongside academic objectives. During this unit of work it will be important to ensure that all pupils feel confident with the main digital tools that will be used to produce the weather forecast. These include the autocue/teleprompter software but also the video capture and editing software. For children this could be presented as within the research phase of the project, where they are introduced to the software and allowed time to research the main function, experiment with using the software and begin to discuss the most efficient ways of producing content.

Produce

The overall goal of this unit of work is to produce a weather forecast video. We have discussed some of the ways in which we could develop knowledge and understanding about the design and structure of weather forecasts. Work within English will also develop more specific and technical knowledge about weather language features.

Children will then have opportunity to plan and write their weather forecasts. It would be ideal to write the forecast script directly into a word-processing package, either PC- or tablet-based. This script can then be edited, refined and pasted into the autocue software that has been chosen. At this stage children will be able to start practising delivery of the forecast. The children will ideally work in groups for these tasks. It could be useful to call these groups production teams and define specific roles, such as camera operator, presenter or director.

During this phase of practising delivery of the forecast children will discover areas of the script that may need further development. They will also then be able to start thinking about the graphic style of the forecast.

There are a number of ways in which the graphics and background of the forecast could be created. Ideally, specific software such as I Can Present (PC version) could be used, which allows children to create background for videos using an image library and/or imported graphics. This software also allows 'green screening', where the children can stand in front of a green or blue background, allowing the background image to be included in the video. Live previewing of the image alongside the autocue text can be seen by the presenter and recorded. This gives a 'professional' feel to the video.

This process can also be achieved in other less integrated ways. There are a number of other 'green screening' or 'chroma key' software packages, some of which integrate with common video editing packages, such as Movie Maker or Pinnacle. There are also a number of tablet apps, such as Green Screen Movie FX or within iMovie, that allow this to be included within the video. However, if you want to create a simpler approach to making the video it is easier to use flipchart/poster paper to make weather backgrounds. Projected images, potentially using interactive whiteboard software such as SMART Notebook, can also be included. These may be harder to video as the brightness of the image can create shadow effects and light imbalances in the final video.

During the videoing process children will have to decide which video editing software to use. They will then be able to upload or record directly into this software, which will allow editing of video and audio. Subtitling and captions may also be included to add features to the production. Again, a range of PC, laptop and tablet software could be used for this (Movie Maker, Pinnacle, Loopster, Video Star). The obvious advantage of using tablets to video the forecast would be that video footage could be recorded directly into the app software, ready for editing.

The overall weather forecast videos may only be very short. However, at the end of this process children will have experienced a number of ways of communicating and presenting. A key part of this area of the computing programmes of study is to allow children to achieve specific outcomes using a range of software and hardware solutions. This multipackage approach will allow development of understanding of how software can be integrated to achieve outcomes.

Key questions

- This lesson embeds technology into other curriculum areas but it is has a clear purpose and potential audience. Why is this so vital to children's learning?

- A lesson approach of this nature has many organisational factors. What are the potential organisational difficulties and possible solutions?

Taking it further

There are many opportunities to create a purposeful learning environment where technology is embedded in delivering cross-curricular outcomes. An excellent guide and support to a thematic approach is provided by the International Primary Curriculum (**www.greatlearning.com/ipc/the-ipc/units-of-work**).

Whatever the theme, using the principles of plan–research–production, it is possible to bring the content alive and also develop digital competences.

If it is a historical context, for example, the Romans or the Victorians, it would provide such purpose and, as a result, motivation to the research if the children knew this was leading to a production and an audience of parents and/or peers or the wider online community. A thematic approach based on the Romans could involve role play and using technology to transport the children back in time. As outlined in both the lesson idea and discussion, there are many iPad apps and software for PCs which will enable this at little or no cost.

The use of iPads will easily enable children to gather digital data of habitats around the school grounds. This could be part of a larger project where sources are merged to produce a multimodal presentation. It could also be used with software, like Videolicious, which enables images to be easily stored and a narration added, as well as background music if required.

Many schools have international links to further cultural understanding. These links could provide a brilliant opportunity to use technology to understand similarities and differences between places. Skype or FaceTime can be used to work collaboratively with a school in a different country. The children would be expected to prepare something about their daily lives. This would help promote writing for a specific audience, and geographical skills, with the use of maps to show routes to school, in addition to finding out about their own locality. Children's knowledge of their own locality is often surprisingly limited. The sharing of the information with the school in a different country will provide a real insight to children's lives and not a third-hand version, which sometimes can paint a stereotypical vision of a country.

A further idea that is hugely effective in promoting collaborative writing is to share the writing of a story between several schools. The idea would be to link with a number of English-speaking schools. It can be just between schools in Britain but, if the links are with schools in countries like Australia, the USA and Canada, it adds an exciting dimension. A story title would be agreed and each school would be responsible for writing a story section. This makes writing very purposeful because of the audience and also generates a great deal of discussion in relation to how the characters are portrayed by different schools. Children will read and re-read a previous section in a manner that is far more thorough than reading a piece of their own individual writing.

Commentary

Whatever the curriculum area, the opportunities for embedding technology in order to add purpose to the children's learning are there. The outcomes in terms of pupil engagement and final production are often very impressive.

Discussion

This chapter looks at the strand of the computing curriculum that focuses on developing the ability to *use a variety of software* on a *range of devices* to *create a range of programs*. These skills are often referred to as 'digital literacy':

> *Digital literacy consists of the skills, knowledge and understanding that enable critical, creative, discerning and safe practices with digital technologies. It is about cultural and social awareness and understanding, as well as functional skills. It is also about knowing when digital technologies are appropriate and helpful to the task at hand, and when they are not.*

> (Hague and Payton, 2011)

Notice the emphasis on children choosing tools, devices and outputs, and on finding or generating ideas and information to present. Digital literacy in this sense is broader than just computer skills. Some see it as a way of developing 'cultural understanding' rather than technical skills (Buckingham, 2010; Belshaw, 2012).

In our lesson, we explored ways in which children can be creative using technology alongside coding, how they can create digital media, find things out and share information, and how these activities can reinforce their understanding of media. The plethora of free and easy-to-use webtools and apps that are now available means that primary-aged children have many opportunities to work with media tools; they can record audio and video, make animations, create online content such as web pages and blog posts, work with digital images, compose digital music and generate three-dimensional models. And the advent of touch screens extends the range of digital content that children can make and share to include artefacts such as screen puppets, hand-drawn animations, choreographed slideshows and multimedia ebooks. The choice can seem overwhelming at times, and a clear vision of the purpose and the intended product is needed to make sure that children's learning is focused.

In order to help your children choose the right tools for the job when using technology, you will need to give them a broad experience and clear goals. It can help to think in terms of a plan–research–produce process, wherein the end result may be a digital artefact to publish and share, with stages along the way. You can then think about ways in which technology can support each stage and build momentum into your projects. At this point it is also worth thinking about how technology can support the many children who struggle with getting ideas on paper using handwriting, whether because of difficulties in organising ideas, adding detail, maintaining fluency or identifying errors. The chance to capture thinking by recording talk, listening to words read aloud using text-to-speech tools or working with images as well as text can be a real support for some. A staged production process also allows time for ideas to be refined and revised, and audience feedback to be implemented.

We will think about the planning, research and production stages in turn.

Planning

There are many ways in which technology can support the process of collecting and organising information and ideas. Using thought showers or mindmaps to gather ideas is a well-established technique: being able to rearrange these ideas using online sticky notes and then to review and add to them over time can make this process more productive (Figure 8.1). Consider using tools such as Popplet or Bubbl.us and apps such as iCardSort or iBrainstorm to help plan a digital artefact in this way. Another possibility is to use online collaborative walls such as Padlet, ShowMe or PrimaryWall to facilitate idea sharing during a lesson and then to add to the wall of ideas from any device over time. Returning to review the wall can then make a productive start to the next lesson. Many of these tools allow images or even video as well as text to be included, increasing their power to communicate effectively. Similarly, graphic organisers such as Tools4Students add a visual scaffold that can help to structure ideas when planning digitally (Figure 8.2).

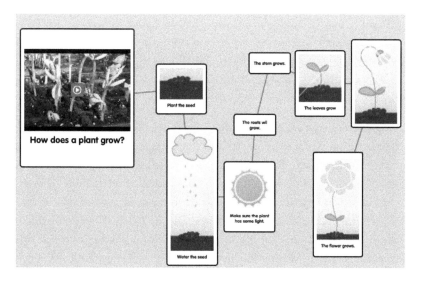

Figure 8.1 Structuring ideas

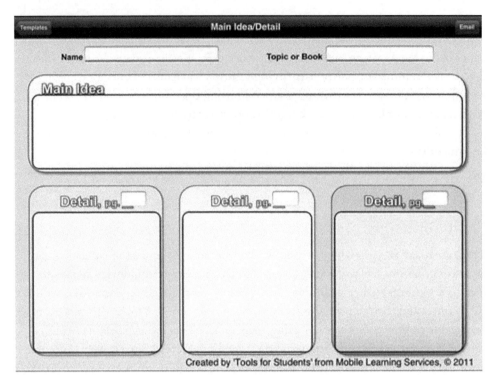

Figure 8.2 A graphic organiser from the Tools4Students app by Mobile Learning Services

Research

When researching topics technology can often be used most effectively when combined with other methods, such as paired talk, interviews, drama, art or simple pen and paper. A good example is this working wall from MrAndrewsOnline, **http://mrandrewsonline.blogspot.co.uk/2012/11/developing-use-of-pupil-blogging.html**, a media collage of information gathered using text, QRcode links to websites, images, charts and diagrams (Figure 8.3). Here the thinking-in-progress is printed, handwritten and pinned. It could just as easily be assembled as a range of media clippings in PowerPoint or Publisher or via a multimedia poster tool such as Glogster.

This ongoing content capture allows children to move back and forth among their ideas as their ownership of a topic grows and they develop sufficient authority to refine and structure a final artefact. Their research may be filled with random ideas, queries and changes of direction. This is sometimes described as unpredictable or 'messy' learning. Joshua Block describes this stage of learning in his classroom as *a mixed swirl of excitement, intrigue, exasperation and frustration* (Block, 2014). Your challenge is to create a learning environment that is adaptable. A helpful strategy is to use talk to help children to visualise their learning journeys (Mercer and Dawes, 2008; Wegerif, 2007). It can also be useful to teach teamwork and establish conditions for peer collaboration that might include deadlines.

Figure 8.3 Learning wall (**http://mrandrewsonline.blogspot.co.uk/2012/11/developing-use-of-pupil-blogging.html**)

When engaging in digital research you can also support children by pointing them in the direction of good internet resources and helping them to be discriminating about their choices. Use link-sharing tools such as Quicklinkr to collect websites with an appropriate reading level that you know contain the information they need. Provide assets for them to use in the form of collections of images, video clips or sentence starters. Such use of prompts, links and visual resources makes it easy to differentiate by providing more open-ended choices for some and structure for those who need it. Despite their varying abilities, your learners will nevertheless end up with comparable finished products of which they can be proud. A supportive classroom can make use of technology in this way to give children differentiated choices and scaffolds and can allow them to work at varied paces (Smeets, 2005).

Activity

Identify ways in which technology can help to provide features of a supportive learning environment:

- differentiated choices;

- prompts and scaffolds;

- varied pace and place;

- visible learning;

- talk for learning;

- adapts to unpredictable learning;

- timely and useful feedback.

Another advantage of using technology at the research stage is the chance to use video conferencing, Skype, FaceTime, Google Hangouts or blogs to extend the boundaries of the classroom walls and gather research evidence around a topic by talking to an expert or exchanging ideas with another class. Alternatively, you might consider the use of green screen video techniques to superimpose a person upon any moving or still image as a background. This makes it possible to develop empathy for historical characters or other cultures, and to personalise learning by enabling children to place their virtual self in any place or time. Think about the immediacy that is conveyed when a screen narrator describes a journey through the bloodstream or the weather on Mars, and also about the real 'need to know' that may drive the writing of the autocue text. Other very straightforward approaches, involving presenting ideas in the appropriate setting, could include apps like Puppet Pals.

When using technology within subjects it is important both to provide challenge in terms of the subject and the use of ICT and to be aware of the tension between the two. You will need to allow time for children to become fluent in the use of technology tools. At this stage the development of ICT skills will be the uppermost objective. As children gain confidence the technology will become *invisible* (Stephenson, 1997) and more weight will be given to the discerning use of information and effective communication of the subject topic. For example, whilst you might spend a busy hour making newscasts on the beheading of Anne Boleyn and achieve a good lesson pace by imposing production deadlines, you would also need to plan time to reflect upon the historical content, perhaps by focusing on the finished artefacts in an extended plenary.

Production

There is a learning transition between children working as researchers testing and rejecting ideas around a topic and the communication of their findings through a shared focus upon an end goal. A key objective is to help children build commitment to their finished product or performance. When you are trying to make learning authentic in this way, the beginnings and ends of projects are especially important. This is where you establish shared understanding and direct individual learning journeys towards a focal point.

Looking forward within the Programme of Study from KS2 to KS3, we can see that an awareness of audience is increasingly important:

- undertake creative projects that involve selecting, using and combining multiple applications, preferably across a range of devices, to achieve challenging goals, including collecting and analysing data and meeting the needs of known users;

- create, reuse, revise and repurpose digital artefacts for a given audience, with attention to trustworthiness, design and usability.

Bearing this in mind, over the last few years it has become easier and cheaper to produce all kinds of digital artefacts using apps and online tools. A selection of options is given in Table 8.1.

With such an array of tools and apps to choose from you will need to find ways of managing choice. We can sometimes be more creative when working within constraints. Giving children the task of telling the story of an evacuee or interviewing a Viking but limiting the output to just five frames or six shots encourages them to be selective about the ideas they include. Imposing a time limit on the production process or on the length of the finished artefact helps to focus ideas. Repurposing information from one format to another, such as from reading a textbook to creating an iMovie trailer, encourages them to evaluate and discriminate as they make decisions about the look and feel of the finished piece and consider how the ideas come across to an audience. Although the finished product might appear simple, it can encompass a huge amount of work as children work together to solve problems, write a script or evaluate multiple takes of a video. Engaging purposefully with subject content in this way makes it more memorable.

Table 8.1 Digital artefacts

Artefact	Apps for iPads and tablets	Online tools and downloadable software
ebook	Book Creator, MyStory, Little Bird Tales, StoryBuddy, Scribble Press, Poster Maker	Storybird, StoryJumper, Little Bird Tales, issuu
Slideshow	Haiku Deck, Flowboard, VideoScribe	Prezi, Photo Story, PhotoPeach, Animoto
Timeline	Timeline 3D	Capzles, ClassTools.net
Poster	Phoster, PicCollage, TurboCollage	Glogster EDU, Publisher
Mindmap	Popplet, iBrainstorm, iCardSort, Inspiration	Popplet, Bubbl.us
Video	iMovie projects and trailers, Videolicious, Green Screen Do Ink	Movie Maker
Talking avatar	Tellagami, Morfo Booth	Voki
Comic	Comic Life, Strip Designer	Comic Life, Pixton
Screencast	Explain Everything, Showbie	Screenr
Collaborative document (wiki)	Google Drive	Google Docs, Google Apps for Education, PrimaryPad, Wikispaces, Edmodo
Blog	Edublogs, Blogger	Edublogs, Blogger
Photo editing and annotation	BeFunky, Skitch	BeFunky, Skitch, Pixlr, ThingLink
Talking photos	SonicPics, PixnTell	Fotobabble, VoiceThread
Animation	myCreate, Puppet Pals, Sock Puppets, I Can Animate	MonkeyJam, GoAnimate, Zu3D
Drawing	ArtRage, Brushes Redux, SketchBook Drawing Pad, Doodle Pad	Paint.NET, GIMP, Psykopaint, Sumopaint, SketchUp
Presenting data	Easy Chart HD Piktochart	2Graph, 2Investigate

The wide variety of artefacts means that children can explore alternative recording strategies alongside handwriting, such as combining narration and images, or photographing drama activities as images to annotate, ensuring that all can feel their ideas are successfully captured and conveyed. If children find it difficult to tie down their ideas it can be difficult to review them and build upon them, leaving some frustrated as they recognise the quality of their ideas but are unable to tether them using handwriting.

Whether the digital artefact is a slideshow with music, an ebook, a movie trailer, an animation, a set of talking photos or a media collage, opportunities abound for sharing with a worldwide audience and gaining instant feedback that can have a positive effect on self-esteem. Publication through learning platforms and blogs allows digital artefacts to be shared straight away. Working towards a publication or sharing event with an awareness of the audience in mind helps children develop ownership of the creative process and sustains their motivation, drive and focus as they make decisions over the look and feel of their product.

The assessment of multimodal artefacts, which include sound and visual content alongside text, presents a challenge and children need to work towards clear success criteria. You will need to make time for structured peer assessment as their digital artefacts are evolving and give clear guidance as to your expectations. It can be helpful to give children a model to help them visualise what an end product may look like. For example, the content and organisation of digital content are different from paper content: what makes a good blog post is different to what makes an effective paragraph in an essay. How to tag and categorise blogposts to improve navigation is an important skill, as is being able to understand file organisation, storage and retrieval, and the implications of these for managing digital content.

Another important feature of a good learning environment is the effective use of feedback and you can make good use of digital tools such as online comment options, voice-recording tools, student response systems such as Socrative, and a visualiser or iPad mirroring and Showbie for instant sharing of work in progress. Try to integrate formative feedback in response to learner needs. With your higher achievers who can achieve self-directed learning, give access to hints and prompts but let them proceed at their own pace. Your lower achievers will benefit from immediate feedback at an early stage and more explicit guidance and structure. For example, you might use Socrative for exit tickets to check on the day's progress as children leave the classroom or to give a snapshot of their thinking by choosing a question type, asking a question and waiting for their responses to be instantly displayed. As Shute points out, it is important that this feedback is related to the learning objective rather than focusing on the child's performance (Shute, 2008).

Alongside day-to-day feedback, you will need to assess progress over time. A useful resource is the Progression Pathways Assessment Framework from the association Computing At School (CAS) (Dorling, 2014). This is colour-coded to show progression from Year 1 to Year 9 against the Programme of Study strands, including algorithms, programming, data, hardware, communication and information technology. You can also use it to determine a 'benchmark' level for pupils entering each Key Stage or year group and begin your input at the appropriate level (pink to blue for primary). The information technology strand is relevant to this chapter and makes a useful guide for developing a scheme of work. You will notice an emphasis on repurposing digital content and sharing with wider audiences, on making sound judgements about the quality of digital content and on designing and creating digital content and making refinements in response to feedback. Talk, audience and feedback are recognised as integral to the successful use of technology as a communication tool. When assessing progress in the creation of digital content, then, you need to take into account not just the use of the software tools but how to make the content suit the audience and purpose, and how to apply good design principles.

Activity

When working with ICT in subjects it is important to think about what it can add. Can you think of examples from your own practice when the use of technology:

- provided more content or added depth?

- allowed for input and feedback from a wider audience?

- made for more personalised and differentiated learning?

- offered increased choice and control?

- improved pace and engagement?

- achieved something you could not do any other way?

- acted as a better hook into a topic?

Summary

We have thought about how technology can help children capture and reflect upon their learning, and offer them new ways to collaborate, make and share. We have viewed this as an organic process in which they build on what has gone before and participate in a plan–research–produce cycle that has much in common with project-based learning. Digital literacy in this sense means going beyond technical skills to give pupils *the opportunity to use a wide range of technologies collaboratively, creatively and critically* (Hague and Payton, 2011). The key to embedding the use of digital tools and devices is to evaluate when it is best to use technology, to balance the mix of physical and digital activity and to evaluate if, when and how ICT amplifies children's thinking and learning. Let your own enthusiasm be a catalyst driving the learning in your classrooms and let your children pursue and share their own big ideas. Generating a real-world excitement about using digital tools for learning is what makes it all worthwhile.

Useful links

Conceptual framework for technology as a tool for learning: **www.tandfonline.com/doi/full/10.1080/09 585176.2012.703492#.UveLml4dT84**

Design thinking principles and theory: **http://designthinkingforeducators.com/design-thinking**

http://notosh.com/what-we-do/the-design-thinking-school

Digital tools for formative assessment: **www.nwea.org/blog/category/formative-assessment**

Progression Pathways Assessment Framework: **http://community.computingatschool.org.uk/ resources/1692**

A very useful assessment/progression resource for the National Curriculum for Computing from Computing At School (CAS). Colour-coded to show progression from Year 1 to Year 9 against the Programme of Study strands.

Further reading

Barber, D and Cooper, L (2012) *Using New Web Tools in the Primary Classroom: A Practical Guide for Enhancing Teaching and Learning.* London: Routledge.

Bird, J and Caldwell, H (2014) *Teaching with Tablets.* London: SAGE/Learning Matters.

Savage, M and Barnett, A (2015) *Digital Literacy for Primary Teachers.* St Albans: Critical Publishing.

Turvey, K, Potter, J, Allen, J and Sharp, J (2014) *Primary Computing and ICT: Knowledge, Understanding and Practice.* London: SAGE/Learning Matters.

References

Belshaw, D (2012) What is 'digital literacy'? A pragmatic investigation (Doctoral dissertation, Durham University). Available online at: **www.slideshare.net/dajbelshaw/the-essential-elements-of-digital-literacies** (accessed 6 April 2016).

Block, J (2014) *Embracing Messy Learning.* Available online at: **www.edutopia.org/blog/embracing-messy-learning-joshua-block** (accessed 6 April 2016).

Buckingham, D (2010) Defining digital literacy. In: *Medienbildung in neuen Kulturräumen*, pp59–71. VS Verlag für Sozialwissenschaften. Germany: Springer.

Dorling, M (2014) Progression Pathways Assessment Framework KS1 (Y1) to KS3 (Y9). Available online at: **http://community.computingatschool.org.uk/resources/1692** (accessed 8 September 2016).

Hague, C and Payton, S (2011) Digital literacy across the curriculum. *Curriculum and Leadership Journal*, 9 (10). Available online at: **www.curriculum.edu.au/leader/default.asp?id=33211&issueID=12380** (accessed 8 September 2016).

Mercer, N and Dawes, L (2008) The value of exploratory talk. In: Mercer, N and Hodgkinson, S (eds) *Exploring Talk in School*, pp55–71. London: SAGE.

Shute, V (2008) Focus on formative feedback. *Review of Educational Research*, 78: 153–89.

Smeets, E (2005) Does ICT contribute to powerful learning environments in primary education? *Computers and Education*, 44: 343–55.

Stephenson, D (1997) *Information and Communications Technology in UK Schools: An Independent Inquiry March 1997*. London: Independent ICT in Schools Commission.

Wegerif, R (2007) *Dialogic Education and Technology: Expanding the Space of Learning*, vol. 7. New York: Springer.

Chapter 9

Purposeful technology across the curriculum: supporting enquiry using tablets

select, use and combine a variety of software (including internet services) on a range of digital devices to design and create a range of programs, systems and content that accomplish given goals, including collecting, analysing, evaluating and presenting data and information

Learning outcomes

By the end of this chapter you should be able to:

- develop an understanding of ways of creating opportunities for children to use technology to produce creative curriculum outcomes – whilst also supporting core skill development;
- design a series of lessons which will develop scientific enquiry, whilst developing and utilising digital skills using tablets;
- understand approaches to teaching and learning which enable children to explore their own methods of creating digital content using a range of software applications.

Teachers' Standards

Working through this chapter will help you meet the following standards:

3a. Have a secure knowledge of the relevant subject(s) and curriculum areas, foster and maintain pupils' interest in the subject and address misunderstandings.

4a. Impart knowledge and develop understanding through effective use of lesson time.

4b. Promote a love of learning and children's intellectual curiosity.

Links to the National Curriculum

National Curriculum 2014, Computing Programme of Study, KS2 Subject Content

Pupils should learn to:

- select, use and combine a variety of software (including internet services) on a range of digital devices to design and create a range of programs, systems and content that accomplish given goals, including collecting, analysing, evaluating and presenting data and information.

Introduction

This chapter will consider opportunities for Key Stage 2 (KS2) children to develop scientific enquiry skills while using digital tablet devices. The lesson idea attempts to centre the use of technology within a curriculum idea that meets objectives from a number of different subjects. The discussion section explores the nature of development of learning using digital devices – attempting to theorise how cognitive processes relate to dialogue.

Lesson idea

This section contains a direct account of an article published in *Primary Science* in 2015 called 'Reflections on the use of tablet technology'. It was thought appropriate to provide a direct repeat of this work within the account of the lesson. The discussion within this chapter allows an extension of these ideas in light of further research work looking at dialogue, thinking and identity.

These lesson ideas will lead to the development of a set of lessons covering objectives in science and computing. In these lessons children will be asked to plan, record and analyse science experiments – with a focus on developing enquiry skills.

Before you start

This lesson idea embeds the use of technology into the learning outcomes for science and computing. Careful consideration will be needed in relation to where this lesson idea fits into the medium- and long-term planning for these two curriculum areas.

Children will need to work in groups for planning, research and production, so it is important to plan these groups. A balance of skills of communication, problem solving, curiosity and collaboration will be key to the success of these lessons.

Things you need

- access to tablet devices that can run the application Explain Everything;

- Explain Everything (iOS): **https://itunes.apple.com/gb/app/explain-everything-classic/id431493086?mt=8**

Or

- Explain Everything (Android): **https://play.google.com/store/apps/details?id=com.morriscooke.explaineverything&hl=en_GB**

- Linoit: **http://en.linoit.com**.

Context

This set of lessons will assume that you have developed some desire and motivation to use technology in flexible and purposeful ways. It may be useful to look first at the discussion section of this chapter, as this will provide a good orientation about this style of approach. This discussion explores some of the wider ideas about how technology can be used to support the development of learning skills that support children in their learning. Central to this discussion is the idea that technology, when used in appropriate ways, can enable collaborative engagement and flexibility in approaches to knowledge construction.

Learning objectives

Science:

- asking relevant questions and using different types of scientific enquiries to answer them, setting up simple practical enquiries; comparative and fair tests making systematic and careful observations; and, where appropriate, taking accurate measurements using standard units, using a range of equipment, including thermometers and data loggers; gathering, recording, classifying and presenting data in a variety of ways to help in answering questions; recording findings using simple scientific language, drawings, labelled diagrams, keys, bar charts and tables.

Lesson outline

These ideas could be developed into a range of ways of designing and delivering lessons. Ideally they would be best developed as a unit of work within science, focusing on working scientifically, focused on developing enquiry, testing and practical scientific methods. An approach of this nature would ideally involve a series of activities blocked within a few days or over a week.

This lesson allows children to study materials and their properties. They will have previously learnt about changes of state and exploring how different substances mix. To enable the children to generate their own investigations they were presented with an open question: Does the same thing happen each time a solid is mixed with a liquid?

There was no explicit teaching about the process of mixing substances so a child-led approach was developed, where children were posed with a question and left to investigate from there (no explicit teaching about the mixing process was given). After the question had been posed, the children moved around a carousel of various materials placed at stations around the room and used iPads to structure ideas and aid their recording of processes (with annotated commentary). These materials could stimulate thinking about (mixed and mixing) materials in various ways. After the children had planned their investigations there was a class review to discuss and address any emergent misunderstandings or conceptual confusions that may have emerged. This approach to investigating materials proved to be an effective way to address the science learning objectives and support the class to participate.

The learning activities

In preparation for the carousel activity, the children were given a 'talking homework' question the evening before. They simply had to consider at home, 'What question could we ask about mixing?' Consequently, some children brought with them ideas discussed with a grown-up. This form of homework had previously proved to be invaluable, as it often enabled the children to start discussions in class with more confidence and sometimes at greater depth.

The enquiry questions that emerged from a whole-class discussion included:

- What happens if we put a solid in warm water?
- How long will porridge take to mix with cold water?
- Does salt disappear in oil, vinegar and washing-up liquid (like in water)?
- What happens to sweets left in a cola drink?
- Does food colouring change the colour of oil and washing-up liquid?

All the possible questions were collated into a Linoit (**http://en.linoit.com**), a free app that allows digital 'sticky notes' to be written so that the whole class can see them on the interactive whiteboard. The advantage of Linoit is that everyone can collate their ideas simultaneously on the whiteboard, so all children can participate in spontaneously reading and reviewing each other's questions, encouraging further reflective thinking. Based on these shared ideas, the children planned their own investigations in groups of three. They chose a question and worked through the process of planning and carrying out their investigation.

The key use of technology in this lesson was the use of the app Explain Everything (**https://explaineverything.com**). Explain Everything is a presentation app that allows users to present ideas using a range of sources (modes of communication) – text, images, video, drawings. It is highly intuitive, with a key feature of allowing audio annotation and recording on each presentation 'slide'.

Once planned (and the intentions recorded on Explain Everything), materials were collected and predictions made. In a class of 30 children there were nine different investigations:

1. Exploring what happens to coffee in oil and water.

2. Investigating how different combinations of food colouring change the colour of water.

3. Exploring how varying amounts of food dye changes the colour intensity.

4. Discovering how the same food colouring changes oil, washing-up liquid and vinegar.

5. Studying what happens to sweets in cola.

6. Comparing what happens when soil is mixed into still and fizzy water.

7. Examining making porridge in cold and warm water.

8. Comparing what happens to sugar in cold and warm water.

9. Investigating whether salt disappears in oil, washing-up liquid and vinegar.

Each group member had a role, such as quality controller, recorder and so on. Generally, this meant that one child was recording on an iPad and others were either measuring, observing or recording results. Every child was engaged in an aspect of investigating. The value of recording by video only became really apparent after the practical aspects of the investigations were done, and the reviewing and evaluation of results started.

Regardless of the role taken in the groups, each child was able to closely view, review and scrutinise what happened as they replayed their videos numerous times. Reconsidering their predictions, discussing what they anticipated would happen and contrasting their expectations with reality appeared to engage the children in deeper and more scientifically focused conversations. For example, the children could watch and re-watch the way the food colouring mixed with oil separated into two distinct layers. Their written descriptions of the findings were also richer. Admittedly this could have been done on a flip camera or other similar device, but the immediacy and ease of (re)viewing in Explain Everything made the recordings easily accessible. This review process also allowed children to 'see' (in slow motion) unpredicted happenings and to replay several times when anticipated reactions did not materialise. Some groups were able to learn straight away from their mistakes because they could immediately alter (and repeat) what they had done to see if it made a difference. One group, for example, decided to see which sort of sweets dissolved most rapidly in cola. They decided to record what happened every minute. However, after one minute nothing had changed. Following some discussion and some questioning with an adult, they decided to review their method and measure after a longer time period and with a smaller amount of cola in a shallower dish. Their results were remarkable, with some strange mutations: some sweets swelled while others were covered in bubbles. This was not observed during their initial activities, but captured on video during their modified approach. Use of Explain Everything on the tablets facilitated their success.

Assessing outcomes

The children used their results, photographs and videos to construct a poster that included predictions (and the investigational questions they were trying to answer), findings, graphs and conclusions. Some chose to write and draw for their poster; others took the images and video they had captured and combined it further with text to create an iMovie.

Key to the success of the posters was the children's ability to revisit their experiment as many times as they wanted: as they reviewed their images and recordings they refined their ideas, through discussion, to explain what had actually happened. They were able to slow down their video clips and observe their experiments more closely; this was especially important as some substances had reacted too quickly to see the 'mixing' process. The exploratory talk (openly sharing, reviewing and building on each other's ideas) enabled the children to collaborate and consolidate their ideas. The reappraisal of recordings meant that many groups engaged in investigational processes that involved constantly reviewing the meaning of observations and clarifying shared understandings before clearer explanations and conclusions emerged.

Key questions

- This lesson embeds technology into other curriculum areas but it has a clear purpose and potential audience. Why is this so vital to children's learning?

- A lesson approach of this nature has many organisational factors. What are the potential organisational difficulties and possible solutions?

Discussion: tablets and learning

Clark and Luckin (2013) speculate about how the iPad can add to the development of a 'seamless' approach to learning within classrooms promoted by the tool's ability to develop interest, engagement, independence, creativity and improved productivity. This paper is similar to other discussions in identifying potential benefits of appropriate use of iPads in classrooms. Fagan and Coutts (2014) present case study evidence of the impact of iPads on supporting collaborative learning, supporting creativity, inspiring learning and helping to develop documentation and assessment in early education. Other speculative discussions, such as McPhee et al. (2013), attempt to put forward reasons for what they describe as increased learner engagement, especially for boys. The ability to explore and structure information as well as regular use of game-based learning features (such as extrinsic/intrinsic rewards, self-pacing and goal orientation) are seen as major benefits for engagement allowed by iPad use.

Clark and Luckin (2013) continue their discussion by identifying specific instances of the benefits of certain iPad affordances, such as how portability enhances opportunities to promote greater face-to-face social interaction. This discussion compares other technologies such as laptops or netbooks and identifies how flexible and immediate abilities to manipulate and structure information in a variety of multimodal ways can promote sharing and learning.

A number of studies of technology use and young children centre on the nature of interaction and perceived impacts on thinking and dialogue. Stanton and Neale (2003) present a discussion exploring the potential of shared computer usage to generate collaboration both in thinking and in dialogue. Suggestions from studies of this nature highlight how technological environments present ways of allowing shared approaches to achieve goals, pointing to the way in which computers can allow interaction that other environments may not allow in the same way. Wild (2011) identified the impact of shared use of computers on the thinking of dyads of 5- and 6-year-olds:

> *Nevertheless, it would seem that shared thinking could indeed be facilitated by planning for children to use the computer in a paired manner within the busy classroom to supplement the practice of a practitioner or teacher who may not always be immediately available to provide the kind of direct support of SST {SST being shared sustained thinking}.*

(Wild, 2011, p230)

Specific discussion of the impact of iPads on thinking and dialogue is usually within wider context discussion of perceived benefits. However there are a number of studies that have included discussion of the impact of the iPad interface on promoting learning and engagement.

Clark and Luckin (2013) suggest that learner motivation and engagement is promoted due to the immediate nature of the interface allowed by iPads. The touch screen interface, whilst also having certain restrictions, such as restricted finger inputs, allows users to easily access and manipulate information; this impacts quickly on learning.

The case study examples within this chapter provide ideas for creative uses of technology to promote talk and collaboration. A number of key iPad apps are discussed, as well as wider pedagogical tools and techniques to enhance learning. A case study of this nature enables understanding of how one teacher has approached developing an inclusive, technology-rich learning environment. Developing environments with 'rich' talk and collaboration is an important feature of primary classrooms.

Talk and collaboration

Several studies have developed understanding of how talk and collaboration can develop children's learning. Collaborative learning approaches can often be seen as indicators of successful classrooms (Littleton and Mercer, 2013; Slavin, 2009). The nature of these collaborative environments is such that 'transferable' thinking and related reasoning and communication skills are seen as being natural developments. However, Littleton and Mercer (2013) also indicate that 'collaborative learning', often seen as group work, may not always be as productive as hoped. Unstructured discussion and group work without adequate purpose and direction will, unsurprisingly, not lead to impact on learning. Children need great direction and skill development to be able to ensure that their talk and collaboration leads to 'good' learning.

The example of use of technology within this chapter attempts to show purposeful tasks situated within engaging contexts which provide good engagement for pupils. Indeed some indicators of successful collaborative environments identify the 'dual role' of being teacher and learner, something enabled by designing tasks that ensure that learners need to take the role of designing learning and information provision for others.

> *Collaboration includes taking the perspectives of both the student as learner and the teacher and assumes that group problem solving leads to greater success than working alone.*
>
> (Garton, 2007, p197)

Indeed, Staarman (2009) identifies the range of ways of approaching computer-mediated collaboration and communication within primary literacy teaching. Within her study the nature of cognitive and regulatory discourse is analysed to provide greater understanding of the complexities of approaching an understanding of collaborative group work using technology.

Thinking and dialogue

A range of studies identify the importance of shared use of technology to promote dialogue and resultant thinking. Stanton and Neale (2003) present a discussion which explores the potential of shared computer usage to generate collaboration both in thinking and in dialogue.

Technological environments provide a number of features, such as engaging animation, and multimodal display of information, which promote discussion and talk showing 'rich' cognitive processes. Wild (2011) identified the impact of shared use of computers on the thinking of dyads of 5- and 6-year-olds. Specific benefits rested particularly on the supplementary role of computers alongside other professionals' work with children – where adults could not always provide attention to children, the computer allowed continued development of thinking.

Multimodalities and iPads

A key feature of a number of the case study examples provided within this chapter is a 'rich', multimodal environment. Apps such as GarageBand, iMovie, Sketch Nation and Strip Designer allow children to easily incorporate images and audio to creatively portray information in a range of ways. Investigations of talk and collaboration using the benefits of recent mobile technologies are not fully developed. Many studies have had a focus on talk and collaboration using desktop and 'fixed' environments which neglect many of the features of using mobile technologies, namely easy and immediate incorporation of a range of images and audio.

Recent studies are beginning to identify some of the benefits of particular apps. Talk and collaboration enabled by apps such as Explain Everything are identified by Wise *et al.* (2015) in a study of iPad use in science investigations:

> *Using the ipads to video and review happenings closely appeared to really help develop observational skills and pique curiosity. Using the multimodality of the iPad to record results, annotate findings, add images and allow video to be combined in one place worked particularly well for 'mixing' as the process often happened quite quickly (e.g. food colouring dissolving in water). Being able to revisit the dissolution processes via video also supported the children developing a more exact, accurate and detailed explanation of what actually happened.*
>
> (Wise *et al.*, 2015)

Certainly tablet apps enable children to quickly capture their ideas in a range of ways, allow easy editing and playback and allow greater evidence and recording of processes that can be used later within learning. Within maths and science investigations this is particularly important, as reflection on processes has often relied on pupils' memory and scant notes. With accurate recording of process and later playback children can easily recall what happened and then reflect on this, leading to greater opportunity for talk and collaboration and, subsequently, more developed learning.

Affordances and technology

Affordance, a term invented by the American psychologist J.J. Gibson, refers to the actionable relationship between an actor (person or animal) and an environment. Actions result from ongoing perceptions of environments and contexts where affordances, or clues in the environment, indicate possibilities for action. A key element of identifying an affordance is when an action using an object is obvious in an immediate way, with no mediation by sensory processing (Tinio and Smith, 2014). Users know what to do with an object without the need for instructions or labels (Norman, 1988).

A number of authors have contributed to affordance theory by identifying types or kinds of affordances. For example, John and Sutherland (2005) categorise affordances into the following areas: affordances as effectivity – where affordances are seen as the relationships that afford actions – causing effect within contexts; affordances as perceptions – namely the perceptions of the use of an object – with interplay between experience and knowledge of the perception of use of an object; and affordances as cognitive constructs – where an object forms a demonstrable change in cognition by the user. Constructs of this nature cause a change in mental representation to occur. Norman (1999) distinguishes between 'real' and 'perceived' affordances. For example, a digital screen always allows the 'real' affordance of touching – whether or not it is touch screen enabled (a physical feature of the screen which allows the software environment to be controlled by touching) can then be considered as a 'perceived' affordance.

Norman (1999) provides a dichotomous discussion distinguishing the use of computer systems, which have 'built-in' physical affordances from the keyboard, mouse or screen, from the 'perceived' affordances offered within the user interface (or software environment). These 'perceived' affordances have attracted more focus when considering affordance and functionality within technology environments. For instance, Gall and Breeze (2005) discuss the multimodal affordances of music technologies. This work suggests that learners adapt and adopt approaches to classroom tasks by using a combination of direct experience and ongoing 'fluid' perceptions of the possibilities of an environment. A more practical focus is presented by Taylor *et al.* (2005) in their discussion of drop down menus and their support of writing in MFL. Their approach identifies the functionality of the use of drop down menus within a multimodal environment to provide a 'scaffold' for children's learning.

An inherent tension when considering affordance and technology in education is how we approach perceptions of 'physical' and 'symbolic' properties and how these are interpreted as affordances. There is also the ongoing tension formed by considering differences in affordance interpreted from either considering software or hardware environments. Hammond (2010) presents the notion of approaching affordance from different perspectives. For instance, approaching interpretation of technology affordances from the perspective of Gibson would allow more focus on 'physical' properties and their affordances. However, the importance of recognising 'symbolic' affordances is particularly important when considering the more integrated, highly intuitive interfaces offered by some types of tablet technology.

Tablet, touch screen or post-PC devices attract ongoing discussion about the specific affordances they offer (Churchill *et al.*, 2012; Haßler *et al.*, 2016). These discussions are allowing a typology of tablet affordances to be identified: functionality affordances; haptic affordances; motivational affordances; collaborative/social affordances; multimodal affordances; pedagogical affordances (audio feedback/role of teacher).

The functionality affordances of tablets typically include discussion of high usability and the integration of features such as built-in microphones, cameras and instant playback (Cumming *et al.*, 2014; Haßler *et al.*, 2016). These features, together with the compounding benefit of intuitive app tools such as dictionaries, allow a diversity of opportunities for learning. Haptic affordances centre around the removal of obstacles for the 'control' of digital environments – with the potential for increased 'interactivity' and 'engagement' (Merchant, 2015). Touch screen enabled devices allow users to directly control screen environments, which also potentially augment collaborative benefits. Control of this nature may also increase reciprocity between users and devices, linked to engagement and motivation (Flewitt *et al.*, 2014). An extension of this discussion includes speculation about reduced cognitive workload (Bertolo *et al.*, 2014; Moyer-Packenham *et al.*, 2016), where users' natural and intuitive multimodal communication patterns are facilitated by tablet use.

A consideration of motivational affordances should necessarily include regard to how affordances may interact with each other. Ciampa (2014) suggests that mobile devices simplify access, control and manipulation of digital environments, thus potentially allowing more developed personalisation, self-directed learning, teamwork and scaffolding. The way in which tablets foster collaboration is discussed by Achiam *et al.* (2014) in their discussion of affordance and distributed cognition within museum exhibitions. This would suggest that the collaborative nature of working together offers 'hidden' (cognitive and affective) affordances, and the promotion of joint achievement of shared objectives (producing a plan/video/report etc., etc.) offers a 'perceived' affordance.

Tablet environments typically include intuitively designed apps that allow manipulation of a range of modes of communication in a range of contexts (such as text, audio, video, symbols, diagrams) (Flewitt *et al.*, 2014). The extension of the possibilities of meaning making (Simpson *et al.*, 2013) are enhanced even further when considering the benefits of touch-enabled control. Touch-based, meaning-making processes allow development of what Simpson *et al.* (2013) call a 'dynamic materiality' potentially allowing 'new literacies' to be formed.

However, the key to the successful use of tablets within learning is consideration of the way in which teachers decide to use these technologies. Pedagogical affordances are the benefits afforded to teachers by combining the range of affordances discussed previously. Decisions on group, paired or individual use of devices, alongside careful choice of apps and design of multimodal scaffolds, are all allowed by benefits of other affordances (Hutchison *et al.*, 2012; Falloon, 2014). As Kucirkova (2014) suggests,

> *the learning potential of iPads is directly related to the teachers' ability to effectively leverage iPads' affordances and creatively link them to the curriculum.*
>
> (Kucirkova, 2014)

Summary

We have presented an example of how to embed an area of the Computing Programme of Study within another curriculum subject. Mobile or post-PC technologies, such as tablets, provide a much greater opportunity for truly embedded use of technology across the curriculum. This example sets this finding within the context of developing enquiry skills in science, and could also be repeated within maths or other investigatory work. It is recognised that children and teachers will need some familiarity with these particular hardware and software environments – however, the intuitiveness of the app discussed enables a very 'quick' uptake of use in classrooms.

References

Achiam, M, May, M and Marandino, M (2014) Affordances and distributed cognition in museum exhibitions. *Museum Management and Curatorship*, 29: 461–81.

Bertolo, D, Dinet, J and Vivian, R (2014) Reducing cognitive workload during 3D geometry problem solving with an app on iPad. Science and Information Conference, 27–29 August.

Churchill, D, Fox, B and King, M (2012) Study of affordances of iPads and teachers' private theories. *International Journal of Information and Education Technology*, 2: 251–4.

Ciampa, K (2014) Learning in a mobile age: an investigation of student motivation. *Journal of Computer Assisted Learning*, 30: 82–96.

Clark, W and Luckin, R (2013) *What the Research Says: iPads in the Classroom*. London: London Knowledge Lab, IoE.

Cumming, TM, Strnadová, I and Singh, S (2014) iPads as instructional tools to enhance learning opportunities for students with developmental disabilities: an action research project. *Action Research*, 12: 151–76.

Fagan, T and Coutts, T (2012) To iPad or not to iPad. Available online at: **www.core-ed.org/thought-leadership/research/ipad-or-not-ipad** (accessed 27 October 2014).

Falloon, G (2014) iPads in the primary school: emerging research. Presented at ACEC 2014, Adelaide.

Flewitt, R, Kucirkova, N and Messer, D (2014) Touching the virtual, touching the real: iPads and enabling literacy for students experiencing disability. *Australian Journal of Language and Literacy*, 37: 107–16.

Gall, M and Breeze, N (2005) Music composition lessons: the multimodal affordances of technology. *Educational Review*, 57: 415–33.

Garton, AF (2007) Learning through collaboration, in Salili, F and Hoosain, R (eds) *Culture, Motivation and Learning: A Multicultural Perspective*. Greenwich, CT: Information Age Publishing.

Hammond, M (2010) What is an affordance and can it help us understand the use of ICT in education? *Education and Information Technologies*, 15: 205–17.

Haßler, B, Major, L and Hennessy, S (2016) Tablet use in schools: a critical review of the evidence for learning outcomes. *Journal of Computer Assisted Learning*, 32: 139–56.

Hutchison, A, Beschorner, B and Schmidt-Crawford, D (2012) Exploring the use of the iPad for literacy learning. *The Reading Teacher*, 66: 15–23.

John, P and Sutherland, R (2005) Affordance, opportunity and the pedagogical implications of ICT. *Educational Review*, 57: 405–13.

Kucirkova, N (2014) iPads in early education: separating assumptions and evidence. *Frontiers in Psychology*, July. Available online at: **http://dx.doi.org/10.3389/fpsyg.2014.00715** (accessed 20 December 2016).

Littleton, K and Mercer, N (2013) *Interthinking: Putting Talk to Work*. Abingdon: Routledge.

McPhee, I, Marks, L and Marks, D (2013) Examining the impact of the Apple 'iPad' on male and female classroom engagement in a primary school in Scotland. ICICTE 2013 Proceedings.

Merchant, G (2015) Keep taking the tablets: iPads, story apps and early literacy. *Australian Journal of Language and Literacy*, 38: 3–11.

Moyer-Packenham, PS, Bullock, EK, Shumway, JF, Tucker, SI, Watts, CM, Westenskow, A, Anderson-Pence, KL, Maahs-Fladung, C, Boyer-Thurgood, J, Gulkilik, H and Jordan, J (2016) The role of affordances in children's learning performance and efficiency when using virtual manipulative mathematics touch-screen apps. *Mathematics Education Research Journal*, 28: 79–105.

Norman, DA (1988) *The Design of Everyday Things*. New York: Basic Books.

Norman, DA (1999) Affordance, conventions, and design. *Interactions*, 6: 38–43.

Simpson, A, Walsh, M and Rowsell, J (2013) The digital reading path: researching modes and multidirectionality with iPads. *Literacy*, 47: 123–30.

Slavin RE (2009) Cooperative learning. In McCulloch, G and Crook, D (eds) *International Encyclopedia of Education*. Abingdon: Routledge.

Staarman, JK (2009) The joint negotiation of ground rules: establishing a shared collaborative practice with new classroom technology. *Language and Education*, 23: 79–95.

Stanton, D and Neale, HR (2003) The effects of multiple mice on children's talk and interaction. *Journal of Computer Assisted Learning*, 19: 229–38.

Taylor, A, Lazarus, E and Cole, R (2005) Putting languages on the (drop down) menu: innovative writing frames in modern foreign language teaching. *Educational Review*, 57: 435–55.

Tinio, PL and Smith, JK (2014) *The Cambridge Handbook of the Psychology of Aesthetics and the Arts*. Cambridge: Cambridge University Press.

Wild, M (2011) Thinking together: exploring aspects of shared thinking between young children during a computer-based literacy task. *International Journal of Early Years Education*, 19: 219–23.

Wise, N, McGregor, D and Bird, JC (2015) Reflections on the use of tablet technology. *Primary Science*, 140 (November).

Chapter 10

Extending computing to meet individual needs in KS2

Sway Grantham and Alison Hannah

all pupils become digitally literate – able to use, and express themselves through, information and communication technology

---

Learning outcomes

By the end of this chapter you should be able to:

- support children with special educational needs and English as an additional language when delivering the computing curriculum;
- extend gifted and talented children when delivering the computing curriculum;
- understand that pupils can use programming for creation;
- explore cross-curricular uses for programming and access a wider range of opportunities for pupils.

Teachers' Standards

Working through this chapter will help you meet the following standards:

5a. Know when and how to differentiate appropriately, using approaches which enable pupils to be taught effectively.
5d. Have a clear understanding of the needs of all pupils, including those with special educational needs; those of high ability; those with English as an additional language; those with disabilities; and be able to use and evaluate distinctive teaching approaches to engage and support them.
4e. Contribute to the design and provision of an engaging curriculum.

Pupils should learn to:

- design, write and debug programs that accomplish specific goals;
- use sequence, selection and repetition in programs; work with variables;
- use a range of digital devices to design and create a range of programs that accomplish given goals.

Introduction

One aspect of teaching computing that frequently worries teachers is how best to provide for the individual needs of pupils. When some of your class struggle with writing sentences using accurate punctuation, how can they be expected to *design, write and debug programs*? Whilst other children confidently apply rules systematically, how do you ensure that they are challenged when *using sequence, selection, and repetition in programs*? This chapter looks at how to ensure that all pupils are able to meet the requirements of the computing curriculum as well as how to challenge those who excel. We will explore the possibilities of support and challenge when teaching programming through the creation of music.

Programming can offer a completely different range of experiences compared to expressing yourself in other media as it allows for expression to a near-professional level, even with a limited skillset. When pupils program a game, an application, an interactive story or an animation, to name but a few, they can make real things happen. They begin with a task, work towards a clear and specific end goal and then, at the end of the work, they have something that they can show to others. The results of their hard work can be shared straight away – and they can get feedback from a wider audience than just their teacher. This often means that computing appeals to pupils who do not engage readily with learning in other subjects. In addition, many pupils respond well to the clear and uncompromising rules that computers require.

Lesson idea: to know how to write a simple program to create music

This lesson idea can be used as a standalone lesson, as an introduction to programming or as part of a series of lessons allowing you to explore more specific aspects of programming. The lesson involves pupils writing a computer program that creates music. They will use a variety of programming concepts such as sequence, selection and repetition, as well as debugging skills.

Things you need

- a computer (Windows, Mac, Linux or Raspberry Pi);

- Scratch (free at **https://scratch.mit.edu**);

- Sonic Pi software program (free to download from **http://sonic-pi.net**);

- headphones (optional);

- speakers (only necessary with Raspberry Pi).

Before you start

This lesson assumes that you have a basic knowledge of the free Scratch programming software. If you need to brush up on this, there is an excellent step-by-step introduction and some starter projects to explore in the Help section of the Scratch website (**http://scratch.mit.edu/help**).

You need to have Sonic Pi installed on your computer; this can be downloaded for free from **http://sonic-pi.net/www.cl.cam.ac.uk/projects/raspberrypi/sonicpi**. If you're using a Raspberry Pi computer, the latest version should already be installed. Look in the menu under 'Programming'.

You need to be familiar with a few programming concepts. Programming concepts that are useful to know are given below.

- Each coding instruction needs to go on a new line.

- Specific commands are used and need to be copied exactly.

- Code runs sequentially, from top to bottom.

- A loop means to repeat a section of code.

- Comments are notes that cannot be seen in the computer program. They help other programmers understand what your code does.

These concepts are the basis of programming, whether you are using a visual editor like Scratch or a text-based editor like Sonic Pi; how you implement them may vary a little.

The last thing you need to know about creating music on a computer is that musical notes are often given a numerical value. This can make composition easier (bigger numbers are higher notes), but it also allows us to make use of other numerical features such as generating random numbers and changing the music based on a number. These notes are MIDI note numbers and you can find conversion tables by searching for this. You should see that the note '60' is the same as a middle C.

The main commands you need to know when using Sonic Pi are given in Table 10.1.

Table 10.1 Sonic Pi commands

Code	What it does	Example
play 60	Plays the MIDI note 60; 60 can be replaced with different values	play 60
play :c	Plays the musical note 'middle c', which is the same note as above	play :c
sleep 1	Adds a one-second pause; 1 can be replaced with different values, including decimals	play 60 sleep 1 play 64
play 60 play 64	Plays the MIDI notes 60 and 64 at the same time	play 60 play 64
x.times do	Repeat whatever code is in between the commands three times. Three can be replaced with other numbers	3.times do play 60 sleep 1 play 64 end
live_loop :name do	Repeats a section of code forever, but can be edited whilst the music is playing. You can run several at once and have different live loops for your bass and melody sounds. Each live_loop must have a different name (after the colon)	live_loop :bass do play 50 sleep 0.5 play 58 play 0.5 end
rrand(x, y100)	Chooses a random number between the two numbers in the brackets	play rrand(60, 100)
use_synth :name	Changes the sounds of the musical notes. When you start typing the colon, there will be a list of possible synths to choose from	use_synth :blade play 50 sleep 0.5 play 58 play 0.5
sample :name	Play a short piece of music to add effects to your music. These can be added into your single notes. When you start typing the colon, there will be a list of possible samples to choose from	sample :ambi_dark_whoosh sleep 2 play 62 sleep 0.5
#comment	Whatever follows the # is ignored by the computer but read by humans to explain what the code does	#this is a comment

Context

If you use this lesson as an introduction to programming you will not need to use the more advanced commands. The lessons can progress throughout a unit of work on making music through programming, allowing pupils to develop their skills and deepen their understanding of programming concepts. This lesson focuses on meeting individual needs through the extensive supportive frameworks.

Learning outcomes for this set of lessons

Pupils will:

- be aware that programming code runs sequentially;

- understand that programming allows us to create exactly what we want;

- know how to use repetition in a program;

- experiment with music while applying different programming concepts.

Lesson 1

If this is the first time the pupils have used the Raspberry Pi then it will be necessary to discuss how it works and the necessary inputs, outputs and processes. If this is the case, there are activities described earlier on in Chapter 5.

Pupils need to connect their Raspberry Pi to a power supply, monitor, mouse and keyboard and open the Sonic Pi application. When the application loads, they will see the screen shown in Figure 10.1.

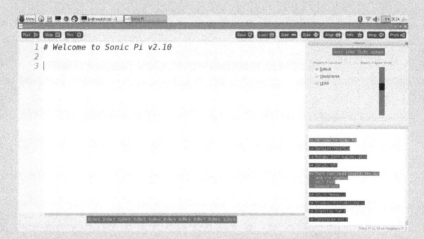

Figure 10.1   Sonic Pi application
www.cl.cam.ac.uk/projects/raspberrypi/sonicpi/teaching.html

- The 'Buffer' pages are where you type the code. You can have a different program in each one if you don't want to delete your code each time you try something new.

- The code will not run as you write it (unless it's in a live_loop); when you are ready to run your code, you need to press Play. If you want to stop it before it finishes running, press Stop.

The 'Log' allows you to see which piece of code is running at a particular time and what it is doing.

The Error Panel appears at the bottom and explains what has gone wrong when code is written incorrectly – don't forget about this as it can show you where to look for errors!

Explain to the children that Scratch has a sound section in its code to create music and the Sonic Pi application allows you to write code to create music. In both of them you need to write what note it needs to play.

Show the pupils the code:

    play 60

Ask: what do they think it does? Run the code and demonstrate what happens – were they correct? In Scratch this is 'Play note' and then select the numbered note you want, and in Sonic Pi this is 'Play' and then the note typed. What do the pupils think will happen if you write 'Play 65'? What about 'Play 55'? Discuss, predict, share and test a few times and encourage the children to recognise patterns. Next, ask the pupils what will happen when you write:

```
play 60
play 70
```

They will probably suggest that it will play note 60 and then note 70. Run the code. Ask the pupils to explain what happened. Both notes seem to have played at the same time. Why? Give the pupils some time to discuss and then explain that a computer works really quickly. This means that it *did* play note 60 first, and then note 70 second, but it was so quick it sounded like they were played at the same time. What might we need to add so that we can hear the computer play 60 and then play 70? Pupils may suggest things like 'pause' or 'wait'. Explain that in Sonic Pi, it needs to be:

```
sleep 1
```

Ask the pupils to discuss and write on whiteboards the code needed to play note 52, sleep 4 seconds and then play note 70. This will allow you an assessment for learning opportunity to check they've understood the need for each piece of code to be on a new line and for the instructions to be sequential. Pupils should write:

```
play 52
sleep 4
play 70
```

Pupils should then be given time to be creative and explore what they can create musically. You may have some children who prefer to create music based on existing tunes; encourage them to try and create something themselves but it may be wise to have some MIDI note number cards around for recognisable tunes. For example, Twinkle, Twinkle, Little Star:

```
60, 60, 67, 67, 69, 69, 67
65, 65, 64, 64, 62, 62, 60
```

These note patterns are not the code that the pupils will need to write to create this music, so they are still having to think about the coding concepts. From here, I would ask children to attempt to continue the song by listening to the music and using trial and error. By listening to what does not sound correct and editing the code accordingly, they are beginning to debug their code.

As a plenary it is nice for pupils to be able to share their work (just unplug the headphones being used) and get some feedback from their peers about the code and musical compositions.

Differentiation

Programming to create music means that pupils can debug programs by listening to their creations and make their own judgements of what sounds right or wrong. Using sound rather than just reading code makes computer programming more accessible and gives children instant feedback on their work.

You may decide, based on the needs of your class, that some children would benefit from using Scratch to create music instead of Sonic Pi. Using Scratch reduces issues of syntax, and language barriers, by allowing children to drag and drop pieces of code. The same music activities can easily be set up in Scratch (Figure 10.2).

Figure 10.2 Using Scratch

Lesson 2

Ask your pupils to think of tasks that they repeat frequently; for example, going to school. Ask them what they do each day. They are likely come up with a rough idea that they 'get up, go to school, come home, play, go to bed'. Ask them how frequently they repeat this. The answer is five times in a school week. Explain that we could write the same thing down five times but this is boring and time consuming; instead we can say that this routine is repeated. Computer programs do this all the time to make the program run more quickly. Using repeats also means less writing for the programmers.

Begin this lesson with an unplugged activity looking at a song with lots of repeats. Show the children an example such as that shown in Figure 10.3.

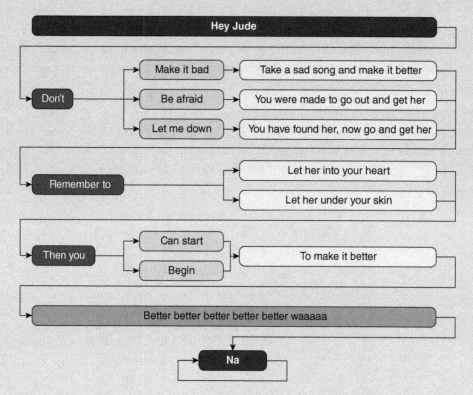

Figure 10.3 Hey Jude flowchart (created by Sarah Emerson on **http://loveallthis.tumblr.com/ post/166124704**)

You may wish to play 'Hey Jude' by The Beatles, so the pupils can see what Figure 10.3 is showing. Ask the pupils to talk a partner through the diagram, reminding them of sequencing. Extend those who need it by discussing repeats within repeats, also referred to as nested loops. Now give groups of children some songs for them to break down themselves. Examples could be:

- 'Twinkle, Twinkle, Little Star';
- 'If You're Happy and You Know It';
- 'The Wheels on the Bus';
- 'I am the Music Man'.

Now the transition needs to be made from the unplugged activity to the plugged. Remind the children that in programming it is called a loop when you want to repeat the same thing. Here is an example of a loop in Sonic Pi:

```
        2.times do
          play 60
          sleep 1
    end
```

Ask pupils to explain to their partners what they think it does. They need to explain each bit of the code, including the numbers and the 'ends'. Discuss their ideas and ensure that they understand all the points. The code inside the loop needs to be indented to show the computer what is within, and what is outside of the loop.

Scratch creates the same image of things in and outside the loop using its jigsaw pieces to wrap around code (Figure 10.4).

Figure 10.4 Scratch creating a loop

Differentiation

Do not worry about doing the main inputs using the Sonic Pi application and then asking some of your pupils to use Scratch. The concepts are entirely transferable and it may be that pupils understand the principles behind the code but just struggle to write the correct code due to issues with spelling or punctuation. Using the Sonic Pi application with your more able pupils means that they need to ensure that all of the syntax is correct. With such an open-ended environment, they can progress through a range of challenges, adding more and more complexity to their music. It can be useful to create syntax cards introducing new programming concepts, with explanations and examples, so that children can independently try to implement them.

Taking it further

Beyond the lessons outlined here, you could continue to develop pupils' understanding of programming concepts such as randomisation, parallelism, nested loops and much more. These techniques can help to make pupils' compositions more musical.

Other avenues you could explore within this unit include programming Scratch sprites to make a dance routine to go with the piece of music, or trying to create a range of more complex songs. Children should be able to use trial and error to find the correct notes for a song if they can regularly listen to the original tune.

Activity

- Plan a role-play activity which simulates a piece of code. Each person is given one line of code; what will they all need to do?

- Create troubleshooting cards for common errors to try and help children become more independent, e.g., Is it all lower-case? Have you checked the spelling?

- Consider the differences that might occur between those who are musically gifted and talented and those who are gifted and talented at programming. How will you provide for both?

Discussion

We have explored ways in which programming in a musical environment can provide a stimulating and responsive environment for providing support and challenge across a range of abilities. In our discussion we will consider further ways in which technologies can support pupils with special needs and also consider how they can provide extra challenges for the gifted and talented.

The learner mix

Even in a conventional setting, individual aptitudes, preferences in learning styles and specific learning needs pose a challenge for teachers, and classroom practitioners will need to have a learning plan that takes account of individual capabilities, preferences and barriers. From those with specific learning difficulties such as dyslexia, dyscalculia or dyspraxia, to those with raised academic potential, the computing curriculum has the potential to stimulate, engage and extend learning.

All children want to learn, explore and control their worlds, be creative and have an impact and most are confident with technology. Many children, however, face individual challenges that impede their learning. According to the DfE (2015) 15.4 per cent of pupils in England have identified special educational needs (equating to 1,301,445 pupils). There are many different levels of special educational needs and disabilities (SENDs), and it has been estimated that as many as one in five children may need extra support with their learning at some stage. Technology has a powerful role to play in supporting the learning and social needs of children with a range of physical, sensory, communication or cognitive disabilities. For many children, technology means that they can be included in lessons and access a wider curriculum; for some, it is the only way for them to make their thoughts and needs known. Technology can support inclusion by enabling greater autonomy, assisting with communication and promoting practices that reach beyond school.

In recent years there has been increased convergence between specialist *assistive technology*, which helps people with SENDs to overcome the additional challenges they face in communication and learning, and the broader field of *educational technology*, which can benefit all students. Both fields have been marked by rapid change. Recently we have seen an uptake of mobile devices for pupils with SENDs, accompanied by the phasing out of computer suites; new devices are emerging based on eye gaze, augmented and virtual reality, gesture and thought control; there is an increase in technology enabled multisensory environments, in the use of robots and drones for telepresence, and in the use of music and media technologies for digital making. Developments such as these open up many possibilities for extending the range of experiential learning opportunities for pupils with SENDs (see Table 10.2).

Table 10.2 Technologies supporting SENDs across the primary curriculum

Areas in which technologies can support pupils with SENDs across the primary curriculum	Example assistive and educational technologies
Supporting literacy development for pupils with reading and writing challenges	• Text to speech, predictive text, talking word processors, software supporting writing, screen readers, voice recognition, symbol supported software and communication devices. • Ebooks for creating, reading and responding to texts. Eye gaze and eye tracking. • Visual magnifiers, screen readers, CCTVs and other devices for the visually impaired such as braille note takers.
Supporting children as researchers and inquirers	• Specialised access devices such as keyboards, switches, mice, head mice. • Tools for online collaboration, peer support and targeted feedback. • Hardware and software for the visually impaired. • Text to speech, predictive text, talking word processors, software supporting writing, screen readers, voice recognition. • MyScript suite of apps for maths notation.
Supporting pupils' engagement with the physical world outdoors	• Mobile devices, cameras and videos, GoPros, drones, animation, QR codes, geocaching.

(Continued)

Table 10.2 (Continued)

Areas in which technologies can support pupils with SENDs across the primary curriculum	Example assistive and educational technologies
Creating immersive multisensory environments for storytelling, for sensory stimulation and to encourage relaxation	• Using light, sound and projected images in light and dark spaces, pico projectors and sensory apps, projected light and sound equipment and sensory rooms, sensory toys, 4D rooms, switch control and accessible devices, augmented and virtual reality.
Making music-making and the performing arts more accessible	• Music-making devices such as Beamz, mobile apps, Skoog, Phonotonics, kaossilators. • Resonance boards and Bluetooth speakers. • Gesture-based devices such as Leap Motion, Kinect, iMovie films and trailers. • Cameras and apps for 3D images and stills, GoPro cameras, augmented and virtual reality and green screening.
Providing opportunities for inclusive art activities	• Gesture-based learning such as Leap Motion and Kinect. • Using light, sound and projected images in light and dark spaces. • Light boxes, pico projectors and sensory apps. • Digital art tools and sketchbook circles for collaborative art and manipulating images
Developing life skills and social and emotional understanding	• Liquid-level indicators, talking tins, money recognition devices. • Switches, environmental control devices, eye gaze and eye tracking. • Apps and webtools supporting social stories. • Hardware and software for the visually impaired. • Games-based learning such as Kinect, video games and games for the blind. • Closed captioning and assistive listening devices for the hearing impaired.

In this way, digital resources and hardware technologies can increase access to the curriculum for some and remove some barriers to learning. The logical, sequential and analytical nature of the Computing Programme of Study lends itself well to creative and lateral thinking, and can also appeal to learners with a talent for approaching tasks in an ordered and sequential manner.

Dyslexic pupils commonly have difficulty in processing sequenced symbolic information and translating text and numbers into something with meaning (Beacham and Alty, 2006). Coding using a text-based programming language bypasses the need to associate text with a visual, and dyslexic programmers often present as speedy and efficient coders. Coding itself is a highly creative process and creativity, lateral thinking and the ability to see the 'bigger picture' has meant that some dyslexics approach problems from a different angle, presenting a logical and efficient conclusion to a procedure. It appears that programming is an area where dyslexics can exploit their strengths.

On the other hand, children diagnosed with an autistic spectrum disorder may experience difficulties socialising and mixing with peers. They may have communication difficulties both verbally and non-verbally and may display repetitive behaviours. Autistic children commonly display an affiliation with technology and we can tap into this preference to provide them with an alternative avenue of expression. An aptitude for the procedural and structured environment of coding, together with the use of virtual and symbolic learning environments, makes computing an engaging subject for many children with additional needs.

Meeting the needs of gifted and talented learners

Learners with raised academic potential may exhibit characteristics that indicate a deeper curiosity for computing. They are likely to be happy to explore additional resources independently and to grasp more challenging concepts with ease, giving an indication of a logical and systematic mindset. The recent explosion of web-based resources made available to all users is ideally suited for the independent and capable learner, offering opportunities to diversify and extend learning in a range of applications and contexts.

For those children who need a challenge, the best way to extend them includes offering them problems and outcomes and encouraging them to work out the steps they need to undertake to be successful. As well as this, children need to be able to apply programming concepts (such as repetition, sequence and selection) to a range of different programming tools and scenarios. When children are really confident, they can use more complex physical computing tools to apply their skills. Being able to apply this understanding on different projects is a true sign of computing mastery in KS2. We will look at some ways you can support children to develop these skills.

1. Using computational thinking to break down a real-world problem

From humanoid superheroes such as NASA's Valkyrie to the role of nanobiotics in the treatment of medical conditions, the field of robotics has the potential to capture the attention of, and stimulate, your more able learners. Understanding the role of inputs and outputs and the potential for artificial intelligence is a good focal point for discussion and the use of physical robots can further illustrate the relevance that robotics have in their everyday lives.

Beyond the engagement factor though, robotics show a real-world purpose for computing and programming. A boom in classroom robotics kits has meant that these technologies are becoming more affordable and accessible and, although these many devices are still mainly delicate and fragile and require some dexterity to build them, they are becoming more robust and equipped to withstand the challenges of a busy classroom environment.

Getting the children to build one of these kits requires many skills. They know their end goal – to build a robot that can follow commands to move around the room – but how do they get there? This kind of problem is perfect to ensure that learners are challenged and developing computational thinking (CT) skills. These skills are fundamental as programming is not just about code and syntax, but also about problem solving. The main skills we are referring to here are *decomposition*, *algorithms* and *logic*. Children must first work out the small steps to make the final project (decomposition), they must use logic to ensure that their plan works and they will need to use algorithms to ensure that their robots behave as they expect. More information about CT can be found on the Barefoot Computing website (**http://barefootcas.org.uk**).

2. Applying programming concepts in different scenarios

Understanding the concept of repetition in a lesson where you have carefully planned the activity (to ensure that it requires a loop to work) is one thing, but for those gifted and talented children we need them to recognise places in their projects where this would be necessary when it is not the main focus of the lesson. There are many ways to do this, but one is to develop 'challenge cards'. These will give the children a program that you want them to design, but they have to work out how to do it. For example, Phil Bagge (**http://code-it.co.uk**) asks students to program a clock. This seems simple, it is easy to explain, but children need to break down the problem really carefully (using their computational thinking skills).

To reach the solution, the children will need to apply all of the learning they have gained so far, but the difference this time is that they need to recognise where and when to introduce it. What part of the clock needs to repeat? Think about the hand movement, it needs to keep going forever! However, we don't want all the hands moving all the time. When do you need a condition to be met? Your understanding of conditionals will be tested when you need to check if the minute or hour hands need to move.

The construction of algorithms using visual programming resources such as Scratch, Kodu and Lego WeDo engages the imagination, encourages creativity and simulates real-world situations. However, aside from applying the concepts to different problems and scenarios, children also need to be able to apply them across languages. Visual programming is a great place to start, but as children begin to understand more they will need to transition to text-based programming.

The Logo programming environment has been a popular choice for teachers of maths and computing for some decades and has now found a place once again in providing a creative tool that forms a useful bridge between visual and textual programming languages. Developed by the Massachusetts Institute of Technology in the 1970s, recognition of its creative potential in the classroom presented teachers with a fresh and exciting programming tool. Logo has evolved and developed various guises throughout its evolution and is core to the programming environment of Scratch, TurtleArt and Lego Mindstorms.

3. Physical computing

There are many physical computing resources designed for the primary classroom – we have already mentioned robots, but this can also include anything from Bee-Bots, to turning on lights and buzzers. Whilst in the early stages of primary school, the physical computing elements are supportive and can help learners understand simple programming concepts, as learners move on to more complicated resources there's a chance for them to apply their computing skills in yet another way.

A Raspberry Pi computer can make it really easy to interact with the real world. You can use the GPIO (General Purpose Input and Output) pins to add LEDs (lights), buzzers and sensors. This means that with just a few wires, children can build their own projects such as a burglar alarm that senses movement and then plays a sound, or their very own light show. For those children that are excelling at computing this includes other skills such as science (for an understanding of electricity and circuits) and also design and technology (DT) (for designing a structure that uses those ideas).

Taking it further

Consider the impact that the primary computing curriculum may have on the school leaver 15 years hence. The stereotypical 'coder' or 'computer geek' today is likely to look very different. Those considered to be change makers in this industry are just as likely to be confident, outgoing and sociable girls or boys and it is the goal of the 2014 National Curriculum to encourage active participation of the entire learning community in the evolution of this exciting field of technology.

Industrial leaders are also paying attention to this revolution in the classroom. Driven by a need to fill the technology 'skill gap' and to compete with nations who are presenting a workforce that is both intellectually capable and technologically sound, employers are patiently waiting to welcome a fresh population of skilled and creative minds. Initiatives such as Hour of Code are endorsed and funded by big names in industry and are set to make a significant impact on the uptake of, and interest in, the deeply stimulating field of computer programming. Hour of Code is an opportunity for every pupil to try computer science for one hour. There are many Hour of Code tutorials that work on browsers, tablets and smartphones, or as 'unplugged' activities. For more information, see **https://code.org/educate/hoc**.

Recognition of the social and moral responsibilities that the creators of new technologies hold offers teachers an opportunity to raise awareness of the wider global impact and the changes that can be made to improve the lifestyles of our fellow citizens. The award-winning Apps for Good organisation aims to provide young people with the tools they need to find solutions to the problems they care most deeply about (**www.appsforgood.org**). The unique connection with industrial experts, educators and young people offers a very special collaborative opportunity and is a model that is attracting significant attention on an international scale.

Independent explorers of their own learning potential, collaborative partners with their peers, parents and the wider community, motivated and excited by their self-development: the study of computing, from the nuts and bolts to the bits and bytes, ticks all the boxes for all learners and is very much here to stay.

Summary

In this chapter we have focused on meeting the needs of the variety of learners within your class through a series of computing lessons based on sound and music. Overall this chapter develops some ideas and discussion about appropriate differentiation within primary computing. This will allow development of approaches to support children with special educational needs as well as more able or gifted and talented children. One area we have focused on is that computing as a subject quite naturally allows a high degree of differentiation due to the opportunities for rich questioning, discussion and a multimodal environment.

Useful links

http://opensen.wordpress.com/2013/03/05/sen-students-and-codin

https://sites.google.com/site/primaryictitt/home/sen

www.raspberrypi.org/resources/learn

References

Beacham, N and Alty, J (2006) An investigation into the effects that digital media can have on the learning outcomes of individuals who have dyslexia. *Computers & Education*, 47: 74–93.

Department for Education (DfE) (2014) *National Curriculum in England: Computing Programmes of Study*. Available online at: **www.gov.uk/government/publications/ national-curriculum-in-england-computing-programmes-of-study/national-curriculum-in-england-computing-programmes-of-study** (accessed 24 October 2016).

Department for Education (DfE) (2015) *Statistical First Release: Special Educational Needs in England: January 2015*. Available online at: **https://www.gov.uk/government/uploads/system/uploads/ attachment_data/file/447917/SFR25-2015_Text.pdf** (accessed 1 February 2017).

Chapter 11

Embedding computational thinking: moving from graphical to text-based languages

Mark Dorling

a high-quality computing education equips pupils to use computational thinking and creativity to understand and change the world

Learning outcomes

By the end of this chapter you should be able to:

- understand the pedagogy and progression from graphical to text-based language, making sure pupils don't just copy code;
- relate the relevant pedagogy in other subjects to computing;
- learn strategies for selecting problems within the scale and reach of pupils' abilities and apply computational thinking to solving them.

Teachers' Standards

Working through this chapter will help you meet the following standards:

3a. Have a secure knowledge of the relevant subject(s) and curriculum areas, foster and maintain pupils' interest in the subject and address misunderstandings.
4b. Promote love of learning and pupils' intellectual curiosity.

Key Stage 1

Pupils should learn to:

- create and debug simple programs;
- use logical reasoning to predict the behaviour of simple programs.

Key Stage 2

- design, write and debug programs that accomplish specific goals, including controlling or simulating physical systems; solve problems by decomposing them into smaller parts;
- use sequence, selection, and repetition in programs; work with variables and various forms of input and output;
- use logical reasoning to explain how some simple algorithms work and to detect and correct errors in algorithms and programs.

Key Stage 3

- use two or more programming languages, at least one of which is textual, to solve a variety of computational problems; make appropriate use of data structures (for example, lists, tables or arrays); design and develop modular programs that use procedures or functions.

Introduction

This chapter looks at the progression from graphical programming languages like Scratch and considers the support needed in the transition to a text-based programming language such as Python.

There is a general perception that programming is hard. Some teachers wonder whether programming is a skill for only the more able pupils and seek advice about the pedagogy for teaching pupils with special educational needs, such as dyslexia, or English as an additional language. I have found that teaching all pupils to program in a text-based language is made easier by focusing on problem solving and scaffolding the learning for pupils. In this chapter we will consider how this can be achieved by choosing scalable problems that pupils are likely to be able to solve, and that can be solved sequentially. We will look at the advantages of using graphical programming languages in conjunction with text-based programming languages. This approach helps pupils to distinguish semantic errors, which are based on logic, from syntax errors, which are based on text.

Lesson idea: practical guidance

This lesson provides practical guidance on making the transition from graphical to text-based programming languages.

Things you need

- Scratch software;

- Logo software.

Before you start

When asked to describe the programming in their classrooms, many teachers will answer 'Scratch', 'Logo' or 'Python', without referring to the underlying concepts and principles that both graphical and text-based languages enable us to teach.

If you are teaching pupils to create computer games in a graphical language then it is likely that they will want to work with multiple objects. If this is the case, then it is essential that as teachers we understand the concept of parallel thinking: the idea that multiple objects can perform instructions simultaneously. Pupils find it easy to design backgrounds and objects in Scratch but often then struggle to get their objects to coordinate behaviours (Meerbaum-Salant et al., 2010). For example, the pupils may wish to make an enemy eat a sprite, making a chomping sound, whilst simultaneously they want to change the score, display a speech bubble and cause the second sprite to disappear. Another example would be two sprites having a conversation using speech bubbles in time with one another. Therefore, the lesson in this chapter will focus on sequential solutions based on maths cross-curricular links that we know pupils should be familiar with.

Why not start with a text-based language?

As a teacher working with pupils from a range of local primary schools, I found that pupils have reasonable success applying their knowledge of algorithmic thinking to drawing shapes in a text-based language such as Logo. They had few issues with applying decomposition (breaking the problem down into its component parts) (Wing, 2006), in order to produce working algorithms to draw a square, e.g. 'FD, RT 90, FD, RT 90, FD, RT 90, FD, RT 90'. However, it was more problematic to introduce pupils to the idea of repeating a block of statements (iteration), as they found it difficult to order the instructions and to decide where to place the square brackets to repeat or loop a group of instructions. And when pupils were asked to apply the concept of generalisation (which parts of the current problem solution might be applied to future problem solutions) to draw a different shape (National Research Council, 2011), only the most able pupils were able to plan and code their algorithm independently. This can be demanding for pupils because they need to learn to overcome both semantic and syntax errors when they are debugging their programming scripts in a text-based language.

These experiences of teaching pupils the concepts of computational thinking and text-based programming helped me to identify two challenges with the approach I had taken. First, there was a need to develop appropriate pedagogy for supporting pupils to master decomposition and generalisation. Second, for all but the most able pupils, there was a need to scaffold the learning for the pupils, by separating the semantic challenge, that is, the meaning or logic, from the syntax, that is, the arrangement or structure of words and symbols.

The 'Taking it further' and 'Discussion' sections of this chapter will recognise the importance of an enquiry-based approach and the need for effective pedagogical strategies in order to develop the concepts of computational thinking whilst progressing pupils' programming skills. This is in addition to looking at effective pedagogy for making the transition from a graphical language to a text-based language.

Learning outcomes for this lesson

Pupils will:

- know and understand how to write algorithms to create basic geometrical shapes;

- understand and explain the key concepts of decomposition, abstraction and generalisation;

- use iteration in simple algorithms, understanding why this is important;

- recognise and correct semantic errors in algorithms through a debugging process;

- apply the structure of the graphical language to the text-based language.

Lesson outline

Class introduction

Ask a child to draw a square on the interactive whiteboard. Using talking partners involve the pupils in deciding the following:

1. What is the angle of turn?

2. How do they know this?

3. How can this be proved?

It is important here to make sure you establish an understanding that the external angles add up to a complete turn, which is 360 degrees.

The next key question would be to ask if they can generalise to use this information to create other shapes. From here, establish that the angle will always be 360 degrees divided by the number of sides.

For example, for a triangle the angle of turn would be 360/3 = 120.

The pupils should now be in a position to understand the decomposition of a square and generalise this for other regular polygons (Figures 11.1 and 11.2). The next step would be to use generalisation to create a whole range of shapes using the graphical programming language of Scratch, focusing on debugging the semantic (logical) errors. The amount of time on this activity will depend on the pupils' prior knowledge of using Scratch.

The next part of the lesson will help pupils build an understanding of the difference between the semantic errors and syntax errors. If the pupils have not previously used Logo they will need an opportunity to experiment with the basic commands. The main

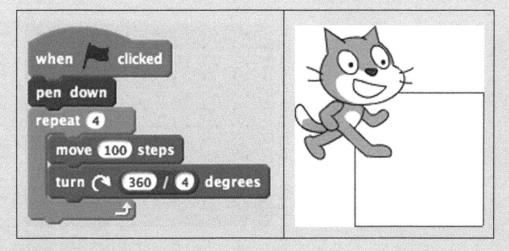

Figure 11.1 Decomposition of a square

151

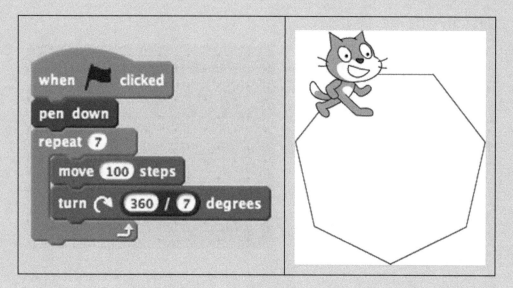

Figure 11.2   Generalisation to a heptagon

commands should be readily available for the pupils to refer to, e.g. FD (forward), RT (right turn), LT (left turn), BK (back), PE (pen erase) and PD (pen down). It is also important to clarify syntax factors such as the space after an entry and the use of the square bracket.

Using Logo the pupils will be asked again to create a whole series of shapes. The starting point should be a comparison with the graphical program Scratch and the text-based program Logo. This should be demonstrated as shown in Figures 11.3 and 11.4.

This activity should lead the pupils into creating regular polygons, using the principles of decomposition and generalisation as established earlier but with the added difficulty of possible syntax errors to debug.

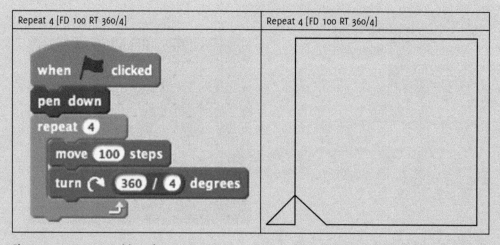

Figure 11.3   Decomposition of a square

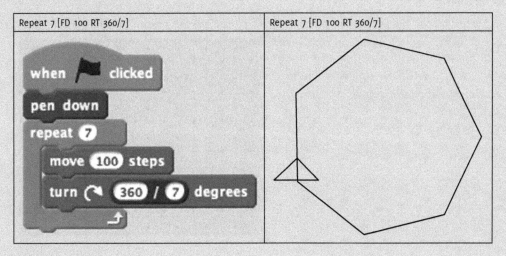

Figure 11.4 Generalisation to a heptagon

Commentary

Despite an improved ability to decompose and generalise to solve problems when introduced to Logo on its own, I have observed that most pupils struggle with the semantics and syntax coding of this text-based language. Using the programming tool Scratch, I discovered a marked improvement in their ability to program solutions independently, even with less able pupils.

I noted a particular improvement in independent problem solving and algorithmic thinking. Pupils had a better understanding of how to position instructions within loops and they were more motivated to debug their programs, by checking that the number they were dividing 360 into was the same as the number of times that the sequence was to be repeated.

To progress the learning of pupils from a visual to a text-based environment I compared the structure of the Scratch blocks to the Logo code. I found, as expected, that the logical structure of the code was the same.

Plenary

To reinforce the relationship between a graphical programming language like Scratch and a text programming language like Logo, the next activity could be a 'spot the difference' comparing Scratch blocks with Logo code. To make it easier for pupils to see this correlation, turn the Scratch blocks on to their sides so that they can compare their overall shapes. This provides a visual representation of the thinking, making the ideas much more accessible for many pupils.

This could be differentiated by providing a range of cards, some with the graphical coding and some with the text-based coding, and a further card with the final geometric shape. The pupils in small groups could then be asked to match the cards in sets of three. Although this could be mixed ability, it may be an opportunity to challenge the most able.

Taking it further

The next step would be to apply the concept of algorithmic thinking to the idea of exploring repeating patterns within Islamic or Celtic art. This would involve teaching pupils to apply the idea of repeating patterns as nested loops. A nested loop is a loop contained within a loop (Figure 11.5).

It is important to establish the pupils' knowledge of decomposition and generalisation first. Looking at Figure 11.5, you will notice that a loop is used to draw a basic shape. To create the pattern, the shape is drawn many times and to do this the loop changes the angle each time until the desired effect is achieved.

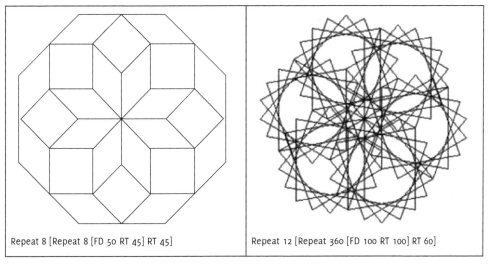

Repeat 8 [Repeat 8 [FD 50 RT 45] RT 45]   Repeat 12 [Repeat 360 [FD 100 RT 100] RT 60]

Figure 11.5   (a) Repeating pattern   (b) Repeating pattern

Activity

Try teaching a maths-based scheme of work using a graphical language and then use this as the foundation for introducing a text-based language of choice.

Discussion
Understanding the challenge of starting with a text-based language

In my experience the pedagogical approach described in the lesson above, of supporting pupils with the transition from graphical to textual programming languages, can be applied to other programming environments and languages as well.

I have found that it is important not to give the pupils simply the blocks of text code to copy out, but instead, to encourage them to experiment for themselves. However, this does present the interesting challenge of how best to support and develop independence, as pupils will often struggle with overcoming both semantic and syntax errors. I observed some vocabulary building modern foreign language lessons for inspiration. Based on these observations, I created a series of 'mix and match' activities, where the pupils could match the graphical code blocks to text blocks randomly placed all over the page. What I observed was pupils actually reading both blocks of code in order to find their match. When the pupils gained confidence in this activity, I removed text code blocks from the game, using their growing knowledge of syntax. Where pupils spotted a missing text block of code, I would encourage them to write it using their growing knowledge of the constructs and syntax. For the less able pupils, I did the reverse and asked them to read and understand the text code block and produce puzzle-like pieces (cards) of Scratch blocks in a graphical code form.

For example, a great introduction for pupils of all ages to variables and constants is through developing their understanding of algebra. Teachers often begin numeracy lessons with mental maths starters, with sums such as '<blank>' plus 22 = 46, where the pupils have to say what the value of '<blank>' is. This can be modelled effectively in graphical programming environments to make a number calculator using variables – pattern recognition and generalisation (Figure 11.6). It can also then be used as a scaffold to introduce data types, such as integers (int), as well as learning a text-based language, such as Python.

In this way pupils can be supported to apply the computational concept of generalisation (applying parts of separate solutions to solve other problems) (National Research Council, 2011). For example, they might turn the number calculator into a maths quiz, similar to activities you would find on handheld gaming devices (Figure 11.7).

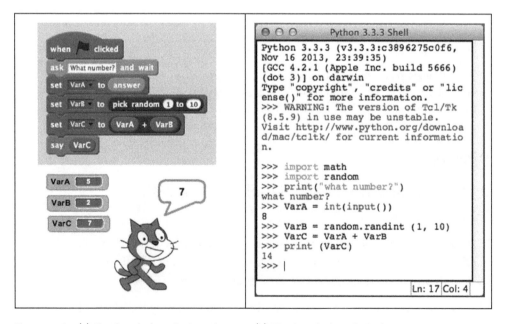

Figure 11.6   (a) Simple calculator in Scratch   (b) Simple calculator in Python

This type of simple program is ideal for introducing pupils to the random number function and provides an excellent opportunity to discuss the differences between truly random and statistically random numbers, as well as the concept of abstraction (the idea of hiding complexity) using functions (Wing, 2006).

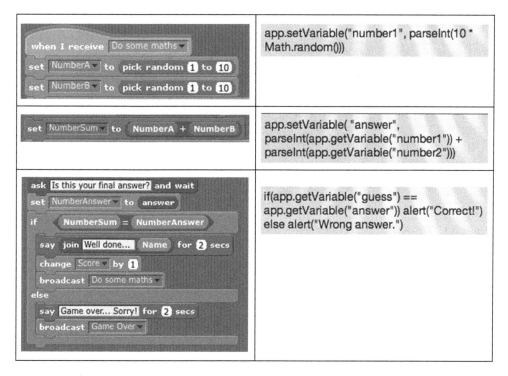

Figure 11.7 (a) Maths quiz in Scratch   (b) Maths quiz in Java Script

Similarly, this scaffolding can also be used to introduce pupils to Java Script by employing a free environment called AppShed to help them make their own tablet applications using HTML5.

Again, generalisation (the concept of applying part solutions to a new problem) can be applied to create a shape calculator maths quiz by combining the calculator, shape and quiz solutions. This also produces an opportunity to introduce procedural abstraction (Wing, 2006) by creating a subroutine to do the actual drawing of the shape (Figure 11.8).

This pedagogical approach can also be used to support pupils' digital literacy skills. Most IT teachers have taught pupils how to make a grade calculator using nested 'if' statements and relational operators. My experiences of this in spreadsheets have been mixed. Most pupils have been able to create two separate 'if' statements, one to calculate the top grade and the second 'if' statement to calculate the lower grade. However, pupils have really struggled with combining the separate 'if' statements into a single nested 'if' statement. They struggled with knowing where to embed the second 'if' statement inside the first, and often found the quotation marks and brackets confusing. Yet, if we use the graphical language in the same way as previously described, pupils are able to separate the semantic and syntax errors (Figure 11.9).

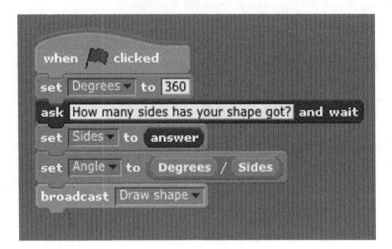

Figure 11.8 A program calling a subroutine to draw a shape

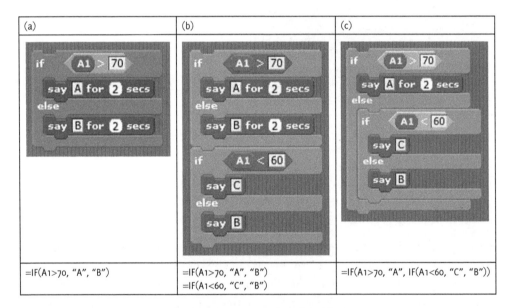

(a)	(b)	(c)
=IF(A1>70, "A", "B")	=IF(A1>70, "A", "B") =IF(A1<60, "C", "B")	=IF(A1>70, "A", IF(A1<60, "C", "B"))

Figure 11.9 Graphical programming languages supporting digital literacy

(a) If the score is greater than 70 then give an A grade, else give a B.

(b) If the score is greater than 70 then give an A grade, else give a B. If the score is less than 60, then give a C grade, else give a B.

(c) If the score is greater than 70 then give an A grade, else if the score is less than 60 then give a C grade, else give a B.

This understanding of nested 'if' statements can in turn help teach pupils to understand how robots navigate a maze using multiple sensors and nested 'if' statements or Boolean expressions, e.g. AND, OR, NOT. The grade calculator is something pupils are familiar with because they often have to work out how their school assignments are graded – this real-life understanding makes it feel like a less abstract challenge for them. It is important that the pupils' learning is scaffolded in the same way when undertaking other challenges. For example, in Figure 11.10, a maze navigation can be presented in a less abstract way by using a paper net with colours on each edge representing sensors and a layout of a maze drawn on a sheet of squared paper.

Once it has been through a design and debugging process, this Scratch script can be compared to a text-based language such as the Robomind software environment that employs a Java syntax (Figure 11.10).

I found that many pupils who have received a solid foundation in programming using this pedagogical method will naturally begin to move from graphical languages such as Scratch towards text-based languages such as Python, Pascal or Small Basic. In addition, I have found that it is important for pupils to choose to make this transition away from a graphical programming language rather than forcing it upon them; it is important for them to feel confident and ready to make this transition and to maintain their overall enthusiasm for the subject.

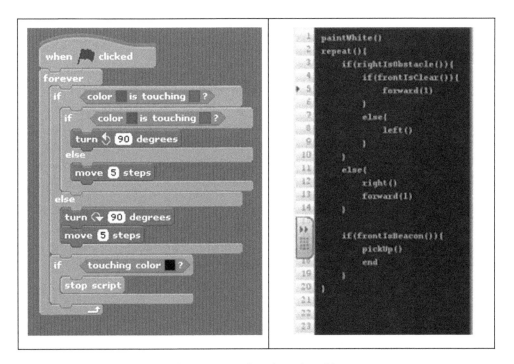

Figure 11.10 Right-hand maze follower in Scratch and text-based language

Reflective questions

Reflect on the pedagogy from other subjects that can inform teaching the computational thinking outlined in this chapter.

Summary

We know that graphical programming languages such as Scratch present exciting possibilities for creativity, freedom and flexibility. However, there is a real need for teachers to understand the concepts of sequential and parallel thinking. This is in order to be able to support pupils applying computational thinking skills with confidence and effectively progressing to text-based languages. Teachers should consider this when choosing problems to solve and the concepts and principles that can be taught whilst developing pupils' confidence.

The National Curriculum doesn't actually specify that pupils should learn a graphical language in primary, only that the pupils should learn two languages in secondary, one of which should be a text-based language. The National Curriculum should be regarded as the minimum expectation of what should be taught to pupils; this chapter suggests a greater focus in the primary years on embedding computational thinking and less emphasis on learning multiple languages and environments. Also, with good pedagogy in supporting pupils to make the transition from graphical to text-based languages, there is no reason why pupils shouldn't be introduced to text-based programming languages whilst at primary school.

I acknowledge that this approach to helping pupils make the transition from graphical programming languages to text-based languages will not work with all problems and solutions due to the constructs offered by some programming languages and as educators it is our role to identify both the opportunities and limitations. However, it does provide a reason for pupils to learn the skills to move away from the graphical language.

Some more able, and more confident, pupils will be keen to jump straight to the text-based languages after completing the Python or Java Script examples outlined here, but as a teacher you need to balance pupils' desire to move away from a graphical programming language with the risk of the pupils' disappointment at failing to complete the task and the effect this could have on their confidence and attitudes towards computing.

Finally, I would highlight the need for further practitioner research to be completed by all members of the Computing At School community. As England is one of the first countries to adopt a computing curriculum, developing new pedagogy for teaching computational thinking and programming is going to be fundamental in ensuring its success!

Useful links

Making a maths calculator mobile phone app using Java Script. **www.resources.digitalschoolhouse. org.uk/key-stage-3-ages-11-14/232-app-shed-maths-quiz**

Making a maths quiz in Scratch. **www.resources.digitalschoolhouse.org.uk/key-stage-3-ages-11-14/220-scratch-maths-quiz**

Making a shape calculator in Scratch. **www.digitalschoolhouse.org.uk/algrithms/289-shape-calculator**

Making a simple maths calculator in Scratch. **www.resources.digitalschoolhouse.org.uk/algorithms-a-programs/163-scratch-teaching-algebra-maths**

Solving the Hampton Court maze using Robomind. **www.resources.digitalschoolhouse.org.uk/key-stage-3-ages-11-14/205-robomind-maze-roamer**

Solving the Hampton Court maze using Scratch. **www.resources.digitalschoolhouse.org.uk/algorithms-a-programs/158-scratch-maze-roamer**

Teaching iteration and recursion through the Fibonacci series. **www.resources.digitalschoolhouse.org.uk/key-stage-3-ages-11-14/224-fibonacci** (accessed 23 February 2014).

Teaching shape and patterns through Scratch and Logo. **www.resources.digitalschoolhouse.org.uk/key-stage-1-ages-5-6/213-art-of-patterns-in-scratch**

Further reading

CAS Primary Guidance Document. Available online at: **www.computingatschool.org.uk/data/uploads/CASPrimaryComputing.pdf** (accessed 23 February 2014).

CAS primary guidance document explains the vocabulary in the National Curriculum and breadth and depth of what should be taught.

Computer Science: A Curriculum for Schools. Available online at: **www.computingatschool.org.uk/data/uploads/ComputingCurric.pdf** (accessed 23 February 2014).

Good teacher-speak explanation of computational thinking.

Department for Education. *National Curriculum in England: Computing Programmes of Study*. Accessed 10 February 2014.

Google. *Exploring Computational Thinking*. Available online at: **www.google.com/edu/computational-thinking/what-is-ct.html#pattern-generalization-abstraction** (accessed 23 February 2014).

Progression Pathways Assessment Framework. Available online at: **http://community.computingatschool.org.uk/resources/1692** (accessed 23 February 2014).

Assessment framework that is growing very popular with schools/teachers. It not only covers progression but also maps to primary guidance and supports digital badges.

Selby, C and Woollard, J (2014) Computational thinking: the developing definitions. In: *Proceedings of the 45th ACM Technical Symposium on Computer Science Education, SIGCSE '14*. ACM.

References

Meerbaum-Salant, O, Armoni, M and Meerbaum-Salant, BA (2010) Learning computer science concepts with Scratch. In: *ICER '10 Proceedings of the Sixth International Workshop on Computing Education Research*, pp69–76. ACM.

National Research Council (2011) *Report of a Workshop of Pedagogica: Aspects of Computational Thinking*. Accessed 10 February 2014.

Wing, J (2006) Computational thinking. *Communications of the ACM*, 49, 33–35. Accessed 10 February 2014.

Index